(overleaf)
The opening of the New Pier and road through Tom-na-Bhoid, 3 June 1898.
Among those in the photograph under the canopy are
Lord and Lady Malcolm of Poltalloch, Provost Doig,
Baillies Howat and Millar, Treasurer Anderson,
Town Clerk J Valrose Clery and Burgh Surveyor CJM
Mackintosh of Dunoon Town Council and the piermaster
William Maton. It was a day of torrential rain.

© Ian McCrorie 1997
Argyll Publishing
Glendaruel
Argyll PA22 3AE

The author has asserted his
moral rights.

**British Library Cataloguing-
in-Publication Data.
A catalogue record for this
book is available from the
British Library.**

ISBN 1 874640 68 8

Origination
Cordfall Ltd, Glasgow

Printing
Cromwell Press

Dunoon Pier
a celebration

Ian McCrorie

Argyll
publishing

Foreword

We have a lot to be grateful to the Victorians for. Certainly they have bequeathed to future generations a far finer and more varied selection of public buildings than any of their successors. Dunoon Pier is a fine example of a structure which has stood the test of time and has come to characterise the community which it serves. Dunoon without its distinctive pier is as unimaginable as Dunoon without Burns's Highland Mary overlooking it.

Throughout the early part of my own life, I saw plenty of Dunoon Pier. Though scarcely five years old at the time, I vividly remember the arrival of the first car ferry which spelt the end of reliance on often hazardous journeys via the old Rest-and-be-Thankful route. Summers were spent watching marvellous old vessels like the *Jeannie Deans*, *Waverley* and *King George V* moving gracefully in and out of the two berths. When I was old enough to travel to midweek football matches, it was Ritchie's Ferry – a converted fishing boat from Gourock – which crept in alongside the pier at all hours and in all weathers.

I remember standing on Dunoon Pier and watching with distinctly negative feelings the first American deport ship, *Proteus*, making its way up the Clyde on a suitably dismal morning. There were much cheerier times at the Glasgow Fair, when it was an attraction in itself to watch the suitcase-laden throngs disembarking for their fortnight's holidays. At Cowal Games, the pier was the focal point of activity until, after the fireworks, the big steamers would sweep in and take away the crowds by the thousand at a time. Like any working pier, Dunoon's was the essential link with most of what happened in the world beyond.

This splendid book brings back a lot of these memories. It is not just a book about the pier but, in passing, a social history of how the Clyde resorts developed and the advent of the steamship opened up both competition among operators and the opportunity to breathe fresh air for the urban masses. It is of course a book for Clyde steamer buffs but also a trip down memory lane for many, like myself, who grew up in Dunoon and enjoyed every minute of it.

Brian Wilson MP
September 1997

Contents

Preface

When asked to write a book about Dunoon Pier around the time of its centenary I quickly warmed to the idea.After all, my uncle Joe, JH Beatty, had been piermaster since ever I could remember until I was over thirty years of age. Almost all my uncles and aunts on both sides of the family lived on the Clyde coast and since my earliest days highlights of my life were the journeys by steamer to visit them. Little wonder then, that I became a steamer enthusiast/dreamer/nutter. I myself spent my university holidays as an Assistant Purser on the Dunoon ferries and in one season helped to man the Information Kiosk at the head of Dunoon Pier. Perhaps, although not a native of Cowal, I have therefore sufficient pedigree to be asked to write this particular account.

As well as the story of the nuts and bolts of the pier I have tried to add a bit of colour with anecdotes that have come down the years. The relationships between Councillors and steamer operators, the infamous Sabbath breakers, the golden days of racing, groundings and collisions, cruise boats and ferries are all touched upon.

The pier at the centre of the burgh is a priceless asset to Dunoon. I would urge the residents of the district to use it to the full: the harsh economic reality today is that sentiment has little place; accountability and profitability are what count. A structure built in the nineteenth century and open to the ravages of wind and weather needs to be nursed carefully. Travellers must show that they value the pier, not just as part of the burgh's heritage, but also as an essential ferry terminal whose loss would have an incalculable effect. Only then can the considerable expenditure necessary to make it an effective and safe all-weather port be justified.

Ian McCrorie
Greenock,
September 1997

(above) Original 1980 painting of the *Waverley* at Dunoon pier
(below) A turn of the century Valentine's colour postcard

The Pier, Dunoon

(above) Joseph Swan's engraving of Dunoon and castle before the building of the pier: 1830s

(below) This print made in 1844 shows the East Bay, Dunoon with an early steamship berthed at the pier built by James Hunter of Hafton

Early days

In the middle of the eighteenth century a small clachan was visible across the Firth of Clyde from the thatched cottage at Cloch Point on the Renfrewshire coast. Its name was Dunoon. Many years before a castle had graced the green mound that marked the point between two large bays: a castle built on a strategic site with a panoramic view over almost the whole firth. Now the few stones remaining were hardly a fitting reminder of the days when the site featured in the panoply of Scottish history, for Dunoon had been the seat of a Bishop, had housed Mary Queen of Scots and the Lord High Steward and had been the site of a ferocious bloody battle between two clans, the Campbells and Lamonts.

The distance from Cloch Point to Dunoon was the shortest in the firth and for many years the eight-oared ferry joining Renfrewshire and Cowal had been one of the vital links between the gentile, civilised Lowlands and the region described by Neil Munro as "the looming land with all the dreads and the forebodings then associated with wild and natural scenes, whose beauty was not yet discovered . . . and with that ghostly atmosphere of a bypast age and people that dwells in Gaelic speech and song and story." In fact the journey across was often very pleasant, the most arduous task being to stop the ferryman giving the travellers – and himself – too much refreshment and to launch the boat from the beach.

Once over in Cowal the problem was that there was, according to the First Statistical Account, "no creek or shelter of any consequence even for boats." If the seas were in any way rough or the wind to the south landing was difficult. Apparently a rudimentary stone pier was built in 1767 but the inevitable storms came and washed it away, while another attempt in 1776 met with the same fate. It is documented that the stones, originally from the castle ruins, were then taken away by the villagers to build their own cottages. The folk were poor and were forced to turn to illegal whisky stills and smuggling to eke out a living. Despite their lowly status, they had the courage to speak with one voice early in the new century, in 1810 to be exact, when they complained to the Commissioners for Highland Roads and Bridges of the lack of a good harbour.

There was an established drove road from the unspoilt land around the clachan of Dunoon to Otter Ferry on the shores of Loch Fyne and the Cloch boat was used in its time to ferry cattle across the Firth. Despite the dangers of crossing in an open boat in stormy weather mishaps were few and far between. On 6 September 1813, however, a 'melancholy' accident occurred. The ferryboat had just left Dunoon around one o'clock in the afternoon with several passengers and thirty head of black cattle. All went well until mid channel when one of the animals became restive. The sea was heavy and there were frequent squalls. The creature, ever more frenzied, started to kick and dislodged a vital plank. The boat sprang a leak and in a moment went down: six were drowned including the boatman himself and a newly married couple, the only passengers saved being one who grabbed hold of the floating plank and the other who clung to a swimming bullock.

Meanwhile an event which was to have momentous consequences had occurred about a year before this incident. The "ingenious" Henry Bell in August 1812 had advertised his revolutionary steamboat *Comet* to sail "by power of air, wind and steam" down the River Clyde from the Broomielaw in Glasgow to Greenock and Helensburgh. On the 8th of the month she completed the voyage to Greenock in four hours and became Europe's first commercially successful steamboat. The amazing fact was that within ten years almost fifty little wooden paddle steamboats had been built for the river traffic and beyond. On 6 May 1816 the *Dumbarton Castle* reached Rothesay and a month later Inverary (sic).

None of the steamboat adverts which were beginning to appear in the Glasgow newspapers mentioned Dunoon: obviously the village was of little consequence. The *Greenock Advertiser* of 7 June 1819, however, displayed an advertisement for an estate within the parish of Dunoon and stated:

> "There is a Pier or Quay lately erected, sufficient for the accommodation of vessels of considerable tonnage. The Steam-Boats and packets from Glasgow and Greenock to Rothesay and Inverary pass within a mile of the house and afford an easy communication with these places"

Obviously there was some landing place around Dunoon but it must be remembered that the longest steamboat at the time was still under 100 feet and, with one exception, under 100 tons gross.

By this time a large mansion had been built on the Hafton Estate about three miles north of Dunoon. One James Hunter had bought the estate in 1816 and had commissioned the well-known architect

David Hamilton to design his home. Six years later, in 1822, James Ewing, a wealthy business-man and Lord Provost of the City of Glasgow, built an imposing home (again designed by Hamilton) on Castle Hill in Dunoon itself. Originally called Marine Villa, it was soon renamed Castle House. This edifice became the catalyst for further development and other rich merchants followed suit and built for themselves imposing villas in order to escape the grime of the city.

Development, however, was sluggish because of the transport difficulties. Many of the houses near the shore had jetties from which boats would row out to the passing steamboats. This was slow, inconvenient and often dangerous and gradually pressure built up for a substantial pier to be erected where the steamboats could actually call at all states of the tide and the journey time to the city could be substantially cut.

About the middle of the seventeenth century the "ferryboat of Dunoon and lands, etc, thereto pertaining" had been feued to Campbell of Ballochyle by the Marquis of Argyll, who had been granted them by royal charter two centuries before. When, in the 1820s, he sold his lands and the ferry rights to the enterprising James Hunter of Hafton – for a mere two or three thousand pounds – developments became much more likely. Hunter saw the potential to the district of improved steamboat communication and in 1828, at Camus-reinach (or the Bay of Ferns), less than two miles north of Dunoon, he built a sturdy pier just long enough to accommodate all the existing steamboats of the time. This pier he called Hunter's Quay.

At this time each steamboat tended to be owned by a separate company but the owners were very often the same people. It soon became apparent that several of the new boats appearing were named after castles and sported the same funnel colouring – black with a narrow white band near the top. By 1831–32 the Castle Steam Packet Company had evolved; this fleet, the first on the Clyde, now comprised four steamboats which plied from Glasgow to Rothesay, Inverary and Arran, ferrying passengers to and from the Cowal shore en route. Their first addition was the *Windsor Castle* of 1832, unusual in that she possessed a male figurehead on her bow. This ship was to play an important part in the story of Dunoon.

LIST OF **STEAM BOATS** PRESENTLY PLYING ON THE CLYDE, &c. &c.				
Names, and when built.	Tonage.	Horse Power.	Draft of Water.	Places of Destination.
			Ft. In.	
Comet, . . 1812	28	14	5 0	Fort William.
Argyle, . 1815	78	26	4 0	Inveraray.
Britannia, . 1815	109	32	4 6	Campbelton.
Neptune, . 1816	82	20	3 9	Inveraray.
Rob Roy, . 1818	87	30	5 9	Belfast.
Robert Bruce, 1819	150	60	8 0	Liverpool.
Inveraray Castle, 1819	112	40	4 6	Inveraray.
Superb, . . 1820	240	72	8 6	Liverpool.
Rapid, . . 1820	136	40	7 0	Do. & Belfast.
Clyde, . . 1813	65	14	3 6	Ports of Clyde.
Glasgow, . 1813	64	14	4 0	Do.
Greenock, . 1815	62	10	3 3	Do.
Waterloo, . 1816	90	20	3 6	Do.
Albion, . . 1816	92	20	4 0	Do.
Rothesay Castle, 1816	95	30	4 4	Do.
Oscar, . . 1816	54	12	3 2	Do.
Dunbarton, 1820	65	25	3 5	Do.
Defiance, . 1817	51	12	3 3	Do.
Marquis of Bute, 1818	53	14	3 3	Do.
Robert Burns, 1819	66	20	3 6	Do.
Port Glasgow, 1819	84	16	3 6	Do.
Fingal, . . 1819	67	16	2 9	Do.
Post Boy, . 1820	65	20	3 0	Do.

☞ As also the Samson tug boat, of 40 horse power, fitted up for passengers, belonging to the Clyde Shipping Company.

The list of steamboats plying on the Clyde in 1820 from Lumsden's *Steamboat Companion*

15

The first pier

James Hunter of Hafton lost little time in promoting his desire for better accommodation for the steamboats plying to and from Dunoon. According to the Second Statistical Account:

> "To obviate the inconvenience of landing steamers in open boats, a private joint stock company was entered into in the year 1835 for the object of erecting a pier or jetty at which steamers might touch at all states of the tide. The object has thoroughly succeeded. The jetty at the ferry station a few hundred yards to the north of the castle rocks extends one hundred and thirty yards from the shore into about four and a half fathoms of water, and has seven feet of water at its extremity at the lowest tide. A pontage of one penny is levied on every passenger landing or embarking and proportionate rates upon goods, furniture, etc. Though requiring fairly extensive repairs annually it is understood to yield a good return for the capital invested. It is an enormous accommodation and benefit to the village and parish."

The *Windsor Castle* made the first call. It was a gala day in the village. The directors of the new company "received the vessel with becoming honour" and the passengers who landed were not charged any pier toll. The normal charge of one penny was actually welcomed by inhabitants and visitors alike as the charge for the ferry out to the passing steamboat had usually been tuppence. Although it was a joint stock company which actually built the pier the ferry rights and the 'solum' of the pier still belonged to the Hafton Estate.

If the building of James Ewing's Marine Villa started off the development of Dunoon the erection of the pier in August 1835 certainly accelerated it. Dunoon started to appear in newspaper advertisements on an equal footing with Largs and Rothesay and its place as a prime resort or 'watering place' was assured.

Six years on and another pivotal event further speeded up Dunoon's evolution. Railway mania was sweeping the country and it was inevitable that the new-fangled transport system would eventually reach the Clyde. In February 1841 the Glasgow, Paisley & Greenock Railway reached the coast and the first steam train drew into Greenock Cathcart Street station. A short walk took travellers to the Steamboat Quay and the waiting paddle steamer. The journey time from Glasgow had been slashed at a stroke and passengers no longer had to suffer the distinctly malodorous river. The 'All the Way' steamboat owners retaliated in the only way they could – by slashing fares, the ticket from Glasgow to Greenock (steerage) being reduced to 6d (2½p). Traffic increased rapidly.

Meanwhile the new quay at Dunoon was proving inadequate and was replaced by 1845 with a new pier. This time it was erected by Robert HS Hunter of Hafton, successor to James, and involved in the building was an uncle of Robert Louis Stevenson. The great writer himself is reputed to have stayed in Dunoon for a time during its construction. Even this structure, however, could not withstand the hurricane of 15 December 1848. During the unprecedented fury of the storm the pier was all but destroyed and Dunoon was back at the mercy of ferry boats until 1 May of the following year.

The *Windsor Castle* was the first steamer to call at Dunoon's new pier in 1835

The *Eclipse* which ran aground on the Gantocks in 1854

Williamson: *The Clyde Passenger Steamer*

A later age of Clyde cruising with Dunoon at the centre of things – this was the London and Midland Scottish Railway's publicity leaflet for their Clyde sailings in the 1920s

OUR HOLIDAY PLAYGROUN[D]

INVERARAY

STRACHU[R]

ARDRISHAIG

TARBERT

LOCH FYNE

ORMIDALE

LOCH RIDDEN

WEST LOCH TARBERT

←To Islay

TIGHNABRUAICH

BUTE

COUNTRAIVE

AUCHENLOCHAN

KAMES

KYLES OF

ROTHESAY

CR[A]

GOAT FELL

LOCH RANZA

ARDLAMONT POINT

KILCHATTAN BAY

PIRNMILL

CORRIE

GARROCH HEAD

ARRAN

BRODICK

LAMLASH

HOLY ISLE

KING'S CROSS

WHITING BAY

LONDON MIDLAND AND
SCOTTISH RAILWAY

L.M.S. STEAMER ROUTES

MOTOR & COACH ROUTES

AILSA CRAIG

John Horn, Ltd., Gl[asgow]

DAILY EXCURSIONS

from

DUNOON & KIRN

18

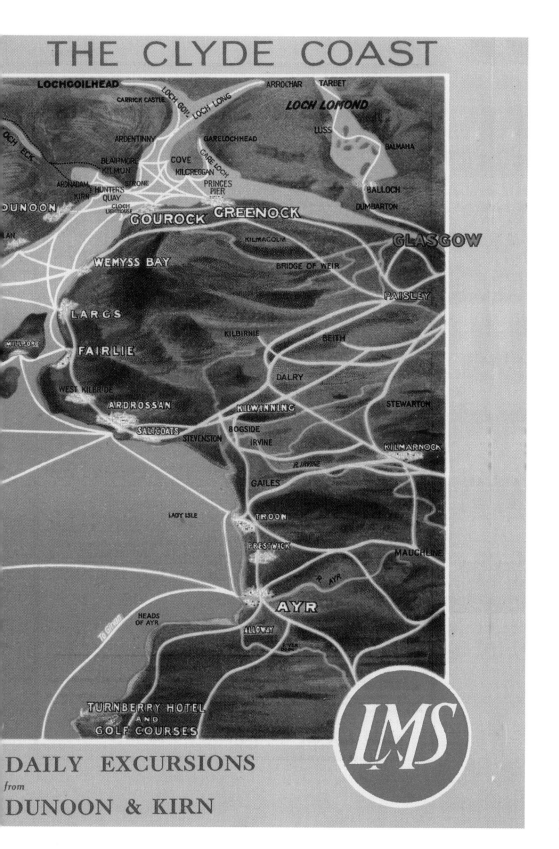

The 1850s

By the middle of the century the Castle Company, now absorbed into the substantial fleet of Messrs G & J Burns, had a virtual monopoly of the trade from Glasgow and Greenock to Dunoon and Rothesay. True, the Greenock Railway had for a few years run their own steamships but they were soon bought over. It was therefore with a considerable degree of resentment that the directors discovered an interloper advertised to sail between Glasgow and Dunoon on 1 July 1850. Able to travel at some 15 knots, the *Eclipse* set out to live up to her name and eclipse her rivals.

The established company put their swiftest steamboat, the *Merlin*, on a spoiling run at exactly the same times as the newcomer. The two crack ships kept up the contest all day and every day and fares were reduced between Glasgow and Dunoon from 1/3 and 9d (6p and 3½p) to 4d in the cabin and 2d steerage (1½p and under 1p).

On her first day in service the *Eclipse*, to stay ahead of her rival, started for Greenock before the gangway was put ashore and two would-be passengers were thrown into the water. Inevitably her reckless skipper put in appearances at the River Bailie Court but fines handed out did not seem to deter him.

The ship continued to race recklessly with any steamship which got in her way – until the morning of 2 September 1854, when "the Gantocks came in the way of the genius at the wheel, and there she remained." Her pilot fled from the scene of the disaster (fortunately with no loss of life) in a small boat to Inverkip, where he caught a passing steamer and eventually embarked for Liverpool. The *Eclipse*, which was not insured, lay on a rocky ridge for a few days, and then, when salvage operations were in progress, she suddenly broke in two and became a total wreck.

The premier route of the Clyde operations of G & J Burns was from Glasgow to Ardrishaig, where connections were made through the Crinan Canal to Oban and the north. One of the steamships they employed on this prestige run – which also carried the Royal Mail – was the *Dolphin* and an amusing little cameo has come down from her first day on the route, thanks to an observant passenger:

"I sailed on her up from Rothesay and remember seeing the Edinburgh postmaster on board timing her calls at the different stations. At Dunoon she was prompt to time, and left while the Dunoon letter-carrier was running breathless down the pier with his bag of letters on his back; but he was too late – the steamer had left the quay, and the postmaster on board stood conspicuously showing the face of his watch to the carrier, indicating that he was not up to time."

In reality the Castle Company operation was a very small and insignificant part of Messrs Burns' vast shipping empire and it occasioned no surprise when in 1851 the brothers hived off their Clyde and West Highland services. David Hutcheson, a senior partner with the firm, took over the West Highland fleet in his own name and from that date, he and the Messrs Burns' nephew David MacBrayne were to become household names throughout the west of Scotland. Queen Victoria and Prince Albert had visited the Clyde and sailed through the Crinan Canal in 1847 and the passage from the Broomielaw to Dunoon, Rothesay, Ardrishaig, Crinan and Oban and the North became known as the Royal Route. More important, the visit had made it fashionable for the gentry to travel to the West Highlands. Once again, Dunoon benefited and this, along with the building of the pier and coming of the Greenock Railway, enhanced its reputation.

Meanwhile, at the other end of the social scale, the artisan class were more and more desperate to leave behind the filth and soot of the city and escape to the fresh air of the Clyde resorts. Periodic Fast Days and the Fair Week in July were the only opportunities afforded to them to do so. Fares were often reduced on these occasions and, especially in good weather, many thousands of the factory operatives surged on to the paddle steamers at the Broomielaw – so closely packed that they only could touch the quay at one point – for a day at a Clyde resort. Dunoon and Rothesay were the favourite destinations and an apprehensive police force awaited their arrival. Mostly, however, the crowds were 'well-spirited' although embarking on the steamships for the return journey up river in the afternoon was a nightmare for those trying to keep order. Dunoon breathed a collective sigh of relief when the holidays were over.

Racing at its zenith

With the old Castle Company disbanded individual ownership returned to the Clyde and competition was at its most brutal. The coveted prize was to be the first to reach Rothesay. Most steamboats still sailed from the centre of the city and, after calling at the various piers on the river, put into Greenock for railway passengers. The race was then on for Dunoon. 1861 was the year of the most reckless rivalry for in that year three shipyards had specially built three fliers purely for the competition on the Dunoon and Rothesay route, the *Neptune*, *Rothesay Castle* and *Ruby*.

The *Rothesay Castle* once sailed from the Broomielaw to Rothesay, calling at all piers, in 2 hours 28 minutes – a record never equalled. But the most ruinous race of all occurred between the other two on 27 July that year. Captain Price of the *Ruby* was passing down river just as the *Neptune* was leaving Greenock; Captain McLean, a courteous gentleman, slowed down to let his rival pass. Price would have none of it, however, and deliberately gave orders for slow ahead to goad McLean into a race. As an honourable man he had to accept. The *Ruby* shot past Gourock although she was timetabled to call (and there were passengers waiting for her on the pier) and ultimately overtook her adversary, but not before she had twice caused a collision between the two fliers. By the time the ships were abreast the Cloch Lighthouse the race was over and the *Ruby* took Dunoon. It was the end, however, for Richard Price: after a further £5 fine from the River Baillie he was relieved of his command and sportsmanship slowly returned to the racing scene on the Clyde.

In fact a new era was about to dawn on the river. This was the period of the American Civil War and, in order to run the blockade which President Lincoln had ordered of the southern ports, the Confederates surreptitiously sought out the fastest steamboats they could find and naturally they turned to the Clyde. Within three short years the Clyde was denuded of its finest paddle steamers as owners were tempted to part with their ships for a very handsome profit.

What followed was a period of greater stability if less glamour. The basic service to Dunoon and Rothesay from Glasgow and Greenock was in the hands of four owners who were also the masters of their ships;

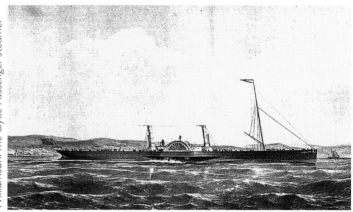

Williamson: The Clyde Passenger Steamer

Captain Richard Price caused a sensation on 27 July 1861 when he caused two collisions in the race to make Dunoon first in his vessel the *Ruby*. He was fined £5 and relieved of his command. The Rothesay Castle (above) was another racer of the early 1860s

Captain Buchanan had the *Eagle*, Captain McLean the *Vulcan*, Captain Stewart the *Victory* and Captain Williamson the *Sultan*. One ship towered above the rest – Hutcheson's Royal Mail Steamer *Iona* of 1864. She was the third of the name, the other two having been sold to the Confederates though disasters had prevented them from leaving British waters. Destined to give yeoman service for over seventy years, she catered specifically for the well-to-do tourist on the Royal Route and even boasted a deck saloon which extended for nearly three-quarters of her length, thus affording shelter from the occasional rain experienced on the Firth.

During this period, Dunoon experienced a civil war not quite of the same epic nature as the one in America but nevertheless one that caused not a few ripples. The protagonists were the Hafton Trustees and the other landed proprietor of Dunoon, Mr McArthur Moir, Writer to the Signet. The problem was whether the Trustees had any right to levy pontage, or pier dues, on the pier in virtue of the ancient ferry rights. McArthur Moir kept up a prolonged litigation but eventually the Hafton proprietors were victorious and he had to submit.

In 1864 three of the directors of the Pier Company (to which the pier had been let and by whom it was run) tried to obtain a reduction in the dues for goods but they were outvoted at a Board Meeting. They then started prolonged agitation among the people of Dunoon and commenced a correspondence in the Glasgow press. This culminated in the formation of a rival company – the Dunoon New Pier Company – for the purpose of building another pier at the Castle rocks, just a little south of the then existing one. A Bill was lodged in Parliament in November 1865 and a great deal of evidence was taken before a Select

Committee of the House of Commons. The right of the foreshore of the proposed site belonged, incidentally, to another Dunoon proprietor, Mr Bouverie Campbell. The Select Committee decided the following year after hearing the evidence of interested parties that two piers so close together would be dangerous to vessels of such size as the *Iona* and the Bill was lost. At this point, Mr Hunter himself, having had enough of the squabbling, took over the pier himself, cancelled the lease, reduced rates and arranged for the construction of a 'new pier' double the size of the old. This new pier opened in 1867.

Dunoon now boasted of more than 3000 of a population. Along with this growth came a strong demand for more effective local government: this demand culminated in the decision to adopt the Police and General Improvement (Scotland) Act, 1862 and arrange for the election of Commissioners to govern the new burgh. Following the first election on 17 October 1868, the local people now had a much more effective voice in dealing with their own affairs, and, as events turned out, the pier was to become very much part of their business.

With a more substantial pier Dunoon was better able to cope with the increasing demands the 1870s were to bring. In 1866 a new railway had gained access to the coast when the North British line reached Helensburgh on the north bank. Although initially a failure because of extravagant management, the steamers run by their subsidiary Steam Packet Company were providing a modest service in connection with the trains as far as Dunoon by the end of the decade. Edinburgh and the north side of Glasgow were now conveniently linked with the Cowal resort.

Then, in the closing days of 1869, the Greenock & Ayrshire Railway (part of the Glasgow & South Western Railway empire) extended their line by means of a long, steep tunnel to a new Greenock terminus called Prince's Pier. This new railhead had two advantages over both the North British at Helensburgh and the old Caledonian terminus near Greenock's Steamboat Quay – it was nearer the coast and the distance from station to pier was a mere hundred yards. The time taken from the arrival of the train at the railhead to the arrival of the steamer at Dunoon was now appreciably shorter.

Once again traffic boomed and the bulk of the steamers' passengers now boarded at the new terminal. It must be admitted, though, that the completion at the same time of a railhead at Wemyss Bay for a subsidiary of the Caledonian Railway diverted much of the Rothesay traffic from the traditional route via Greenock and Dunoon. The Sou'-West, however, gained a further advantage in 1876 when they opened their new Glasgow terminus, St Enoch, right in the commercial heart of the city. The main down train of the day left at 4.03 pm and the connecting steamer – Captain Williamson's flier *Sultan* – was due to reach Dunoon by 5.08 pm, only 65 minutes later. The *Sultan's* consort *Sultana* actually left Prince's Pier at the same time but sailed direct to Innellan and Rothesay to compete more effectively with the Wemyss Bay steamer.

The fleet of the said Captain Williamson was involved in several incidents at Dunoon Pier around this time. During the Glasgow Fair of 1879, Captain Duncan Dewar of the *Marquis of Lorne* beat Williamson's *Sultan* to the pier by 300 yards. Not to be outdone, however, the skipper of the *Sultan* came alongside the *Lorne's* paddle box and started disembarking his passengers. When Dewar protested in fairly colourful language the *Sultan's* master and purser laid hands on him – earning a subsequent fine in court.

A further fine of three guineas came in July 1883 when Captain John Williamson was found guilty of smashing the bow of his command, the *Sultana*, into the starboard side of a rival ship, the *Guinevere*, as they both raced for Dunoon Pier. Only one month later the skipper of Williamson's flagship *Viceroy* was again accused of arrogant recklessness when he almost destroyed the paddle box of the North British flier *Guy Mannering* as they tussled for the berth at Dunoon in stormy conditions.

By the 1880s, however, these ships were becoming decidedly old-fashioned because Clyde steamer travel had been revolutionised by the appearance of three paddle steamers which were quite simply in a different class. As a competitor to Hutcheson's favourite steamer *Iona* on the daily run from Glasgow to Loch Fyne the *Lord of the Isles* had appeared in 1877. At 18 knots she was faster and her accommodation more palatial; in addition she sailed all the way to Inveraray and this appealed to the merchant class tourist.

GLASGOW & THE COAST,

Via GLASGOW & SOUTH-WESTERN and CALEDONIAN RAILWAYS, AND SWIFT STEAMERS

"Viceroy," "Sultana," & "Sultan."

TO THE COAST.

Steamers leave	Sultana A.M.	Viceroy P.M.	Sultan P.M.	Sultana P.M.	Sultana, Saturdays only P.M.	P.M.
GLASGOW · · · · · at	—	2 0	2 40	—	—	—
Trains leave { Central, ·	10 0	—	4 0	4 0	—	—
Glasgow { St. Enoch, ·	10 5	3 5	4 5	4 5	1 0	8 0
Steamers leave						
GREENOCK, · · · · ·	10 50	3 50	4 45	4 45	—	—
Prince's Pier, · · · ·	11 0	4 0	4 55	4 55	1 50	8 45
Gourock, · · · arrive ·	—	4 50	—	—	—	—
Hunter's Quay, · · · ·	—	—	—	—	—	—
Kirn, · · · · · ·	11 25	4 25	5 15	Direct to	2 10	9 10
Dunoon, · · · · · ·	11 30	4 30	5 25	Innell'n	2 15	9 15
Innellan, · · · · · ·	11 45	4 45	5 40	5 25	2 30	9 20
Craigmore, · · · · ·	12 5 PM	5 10	6 5	5 45	2 50	9 50
ROTHESAY, · · · · ·	12 10	5 13	6 10	5 48	2 53	9 53
Port-Bannatyne, · · · ·	12 20	5 30	d6 20	6 0	—	10 5
Colintraive, · · · · ·	—	6 0	—	e6 20	—	—
Tighnabruaich, · · · ·	—	6 15	—	e6 30	—	—
Auchenlochan, · · · ·	—	6 20	—	e6 35	—	—
Kames, · · · · · ·	—	6 25	—	e6 40	—	—
Ormidale, · · · · ·	—	6 45	—	—	—	—

d Saturdays excepted.   *e Fridays only, on and after 1st July.*

FROM THE COAST.

Steamers leave	S'tan A.M.	S'tana A.M.	V'roy A.M.	S'tan A.M.	S'tana P.M.	Sultana, Sat'day only P.M.	P.M.	S'tan P.M.
Ormidale, · · · · · at	Mon. only	a6 0	6 45	—	—	—	—	Sat. only
Kames, · · · · · ·		a6 15	7 15	—	—	—	—	
Auchenlochan, · · · ·	—	a6 20	7 20	—	—	—	—	
Tighnabruaich, · · · ·	—	a6 30	7 30	—	—	—	—	
Colintraive, · · · · ·	—	a6 40	7 45	—	—	—	—	
Port-Bannatyne · · · ·	—	7 15	8 15	b9 10	c2 40	12 20	6 5	—
ROTHESAY, · · · · ·	—	7 30	8 40	b9 30	3 0	12 15	7 0	6 30
Craigmore, · · · · ·	—	7 33	8 43	b9 33	3 3	12 19	7 3	6 33
Innellan, · · · · · ·	—	7 53	9 0	b9 55	3 20	12 50	7 20	6 45
Dunoon, · · · · · ·	6 45	8 10	9 20	10 10	3 35	1 5	7 35	7 0
Kirn, · · · · · ·	6 35	8 13	9 25	10 15	3 40	1 10	7 40	7 5
Hunter's Quay, · · · ·	6 30	—	9 30	10 20	—	—	—	—
Gourock, · · · · ·	7 0	—	9 45	10 35	—	—	—	7 20
Trains leave { Prin. Pier,	7 30	8 38	10 15	11 15	4 15	2 15	8 40	8 20
GREENOCK { Caledonian,	—	9 0	10 30	11 30	4 40	—	—	8 40
Trains arrive { St. Enoch,	8 20	9 25	11 6	12 15	5 10	3 10	9 30	9 19
GLASGOW { Central, ·	—	9 46	11 20	12 30	5 32	—	—	9 31
Glasgow Steamers arrive,	—	—	11 45	12 45	—	—	—	9 50

a Mondays only.   *b Mondays excepted.*   *c Mondays, Wednesdays, and Fridays on and after 15th June.*

NOTE. —Steamer Sultana goes direct from Dunoon to Innellan on Monday mornings. Steamer in connection with 8.38 a.m. Train leaves Dunoon and Kirn five minutes earlier on Mondays.

THE POPULAR NEW EXCURSION ROUTE.

By the Swift Steamer "SULTANA." Weather Favourable.
(Train from Edinburgh to Greenock, via North British Railway, at 7·45 a.m.; Trains from Glasgow, Central Station, 10·0 a.m., and St. Enoch, 10·5 a.m.)
From GREENOCK at 10·50 a.m., calling at Gourock, Kirn, Dunoon, Innellan, Craigmore, Rothesay, and Port-Bannatyne, thence ROUND THE ISLAND OF BUTE, calling at Tighnabruaich, on Tuesdays, Thursdays, and Saturdays; and on Mondays, Wednesdays, and Fridays, to ORMIDALE, allowing Passengers fully an hour on shore, and returning to Greenock for 4·45 p.m. train to Glasgow, and 5·40 p.m. through train to Edinburgh.
Passengers on Saturdays after sailing round Bute, can break the journey at Rothesay, and have four hours ashore, and return by 7·0 p.m. Steamer.

RETURN FARES—

	Cabin.	Steer.		Cabin.	Steer.
From Greenock or Gourock and			From Rothesay, · ·	1s 0d	0s 9d
Round Island of Bute,	2s 0d	1s 6d	Tighnabruaich, ·	1s 0d	0s 9d
Kirn, Dunoon, or Innellan,	1s 6d	1s 0d	Fares to Ormidale same as above.		

N.B.—Passengers from Colintraive and Tighnabruaich going round the Island, can return from Rothesay per Steamer "VICEROY."

The Glasgow & South Western Railway scored over their opponents when they opened St Enoch station in 1876. Passengers could catch the 4.03 train in Glasgow city centre and disembark at Dunoon from the *Sultan* only 65 minutes later

Steamers became ever faster and more comfortable.
The Lord of the Isles (above, at Dunoon Pier) appeared in 1877. She
achieved 18 knots and her accommodation was the last word in luxury

Not to be outdone, David MacBrayne, who now controlled David
Hutcheson & Co and soon was to operate the firm in his own name,
had built in 1878 a vessel which completely outclassed her rival – the
magnificent *Columba*. With a length of over 300 feet, her saloons for
the first time in a Clyde steamer extended to the full width of the hull,
with unsurpassed facilites (including a post office and barber's shop)
and with a speed of 19 knots, she was the undoubted Queen of the
Clyde.

As an incentive to boost the traffic of the *Lord of the Isles*, MT
Clark, her manager, set up a circular tour with Dunoon as a focal point.
Passengers travelled from Glasgow to Dunoon and there boarded horse-
drawn coaches with postillions clad in scarlet for the eight mile journey
to Inverchapel at the south end of Loch Eck. There they transferred to
the newly built little screw steamer *Fairy Queen* for a journey up the
loch to its head where they boarded yet another coach for the onward
journey to a new pier at Strachur on the shores of Loch Fyne. The *Lord
of the Isles* would soon come alongside and allow them to complete the
journey to Inveraray. This "Famed Loch Eck Tour", actually a revival
of an earlier excursion via Kilmun, remained popular for nearly half a
century.

Two years later, in 1880, yet another 'tourist class' steamer
appeared, not quite as spectacular as the others but fascinating in her

One of many excursions in the 1880s was the trip from Glasgow to Dunoon, then by coach to Inverchapel, up Loch Eck on the *Fairy Queen* (right) and on to Strachur and Inveraray. The famed Loch Eck Tour was popular for half a century

own way. This was the *Ivanhoe*, the boat run on 'teetotal' principles to combat the drunkenness which was commonplace on Clyde steamers. Captained by James Williamson, son of Captain Alex of the 'Turkish' fleet, she looked more like a private yacht than an excursion steamer, and became very popular on the route to Arran via the Kyles of Bute. Each of the three new steamers graced Dunoon twice a day, on the down run between 9.30 and 10 in the morning and on the up run between 4 and 6 in the afternoon.

In 1882, the North British Railway opened a new terminal at Craigendoran about a mile east of Helensburgh and set about providing a fleet of steamers better able to compete with their south bank rivals. Naming their ships after characters in Sir Walter Scott's novels, they owned two of the swiftest paddlers on the Firth, the *Guy Mannering* and the *Jeanie Deans*. On 31 July 1887 the latter had a tussle with the great *Columba*. The MacBrayne ship was late so that they both left Rothesay about four o'clock in the afternoon. Opposite Craigmore, about a mile from Rothesay, they were almost level. Both captains and engineers were bent on a race and their excitement soon communicated

The *Ivanhoe* (right) was run on teetotal principles to combat the drunkenness that was becoming commonplace on Clyde steamers

The original vessel in the North British fleet, the *Dandie Dinmont* at Dunoon: ca 1880

itself to the passengers. For a time it looked like a dead heat but the *Jeanie Deans* gradually forged ahead and showed such a remarkable turn of speed that she crossed the bows of her rival and steamed in front with a decided lead. As the two approached Dunoon Pier the pennants of the *Columba* were brought down to half mast as a signal of defeat. But showing a graciousness seldom witnessed, the master of the *Jeanie Deans* ordered his ship to lay to and allow "Mr Mac-Brayne's floating palace" to get the pier first so as not to delay the mail.

While the glamorous passenger steamers received high profile in the press there was another type of steamship whose work was just as essential for the wellbeing of the coast resorts – the cargo or goods steamers. In the late 1880s three companies provided this lowly but crucial service. David MacBrayne still operated the ancient wooden paddler *Inveraray Castle*, which reached her golden jubilee in 1889. This graceful craft, with single funnel abaft the paddle box, used to leave Glasgow every second morning at six o'clock for Ardrishaig and Inveraray. Her passage was unhurried and ample time was given for discharging cargo at the coast resorts. She would usually berth up the north side of the pier at Dunoon on her way down firth and would work her freight by means of a derrick on board. She did carry passengers but it was made clear to them that the return portion of their tickets could not be used on board the *Columba* or *Iona*. Every other morning it was the *Minard Castle* that would bring down the goods from the city. Owned by a group of merchants and farmers from Lochfyneside, she was a more modern screw steamer but with equally tasteful lines. Preceding her down on Tuesdays, Thursdays and Saturdays, having left Glasgow at 4 am, was Messrs Hill's *Bute*, a rather smaller vessel whose ultimate destination was Cumbrae and Arran.

Possibly the earliest photograph of Dunoon pier with Hutcheson's *Iona*: 1870s

Safety first

With the speed of the Clyde vessels and the competitiveness of the different owners increasing safety considerations were becoming paramount. There was no method of regulating the arrival of steamers approaching the piers at the same time. Each master was out for himself and sometimes when three or more ships were heading for a pier together disaster loomed. One writer described the occasion as an "unrestricted scrimmage for the berth".

Following the Clyde Navigation Act of March 1887 competitive designs were sought for pier signals which could bring an end to this state of affairs. Different experiments were tried out at Dunoon, together with Craigmore, Innellan, Kilcreggan and Kirn Piers. Eventually the ideas of one Charles Allan, as exhibited at Innellan, were chosen but it was a further eighteen months before the signalling apparatus was built on to thirty-three piers on the lochs and firth, including, of course, Dunoon. From 29 March 1889 Bye Laws made it compulsory to employ the signalling system and the introduction by and large achieved its aim, effectively putting an end to the risks run by rival masters in their anxiety to be first to the 'winning post'. According to Captain James Williamson in *The Clyde Passenger Steamer*:

"The Signalling Apparatus, as shown in the diagram, consists of a triangular box raised above the level of the pier to such height as is necessary. One corner of the box faces the water, and the two adjoining sides are set at the most suitable angle

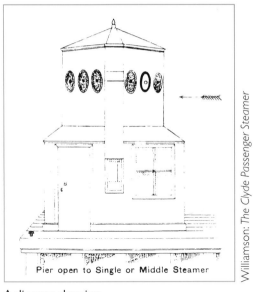

Williamson: The Clyde Passenger Steamer

Pier open to Single or Middle Steamer

A diagram showing the operation of the new pier signals installed in 1888

for each particular pier, so as to face the line of approach of steamers to each side of the pier. The sides of the box are painted white, and each exposed side contains three circular openings in a horizontal row, the edges of the openings being painted black. Behind each of these openings, a sliding board is arranged to show through the openings, black when let down and white when pulled up. The black parts have small red glass centres, and the white parts have white glass centres.

"The intention is that the row of three discs facing approaching steamers should be the signals to three steamers, approaching in these relative positions, namely, the inshore signal for the inshore steamer, the middle signal for the middle steamer, and the outside signal for the outside steamer."

The jetty at Dunoon for embarking on the Cloch ferry: around 1900. This ferry – as can be seen, an open boat – ran until the 1940s

The Motor Boat, Dunoon

Gregor Roy collection

(opposite) The Caledonian Steam Packet Company's new steamer *Marchioness of Breadalbane* at Dunoon in the early 1890s. Having opened the railhead at Gourock in 1889, the Caledonian Railway had made travelling time from Glasgow even shorter. Increased traffic made the need for more berthing space all the greater

The new route from Gourock

The Dunoon Commissioners did not sit back and idly watch events unfold. In April 1881 a rumour went round the burgh that the Hafton Trustees had agreed to make very extensive alterations to Dunoon Pier and intended to float a limited liability company. The Trustees did come up with a price of £30,000 for the pier as a going concern (shareholders receiving 6%) but the Commissioners, understandably, baulked at the idea of spending this amount of money and the idea did not progress. One writer has suggested that at this time the Trustees went ahead themselves with the alterations but there is no evidence to verify this. It is certain, however, that relationships between Commissioners and Trustees were at a low ebb. Apparently parties seeing friends off at the pier were now being charged the penny

pier dues and a stern letter went to the Trustees on the matter.

The Commissioners then turned their attention to the Caledonian Railway. For some years the Company had toyed with the idea of extending their Greenock line over three miles down the coast to Gourock but no action had been taken. By now the Sou'-West through Prince's Pier had very much the lion's share of railway connection traffic to Dunoon and the other resorts and the only way they could be checked would be by building a railhead conveniently situated closer to the coast resorts. The Dunoon representatives saw that this would benefit them and they were in the forefront of negotiations to persuade the Railway Company to advance to Gourock. When plans were drawn up they were, of course, vehemently opposed by the Greenock Harbour Trust and by the G & SW Railway. To try to mollify the Greenockians who, it can be appreciated, did not wish a railway line constructed along the seafront, they proposed an ambitious scheme involving extensive tunnelling. When in 1884 this scheme went before Parliament – enthusiastically supported by Dunoon – the opposition petitioned on their own behalf with alternative proposals. The Caley won the day. Excavations soon started and by 1889 the new railway had emerged sweeping down to a magnificent new terminus beside a wooden steamer wharf half a mile long.

Meanwhile the Dunoon Commissioners had approached the Caledonian to find out what facilities they intended to give Dunoon when the Gourock route opened. They had the visionary proposal of an hourly ferry service between the two piers. That particular proposition took another sixty years to be implemented. The Commissioners were also very conscious of a possible railway monopoly, in that they might have a sparser service and pay more for it. In 1888 Dunoon had in summer 47 connections with Glasgow, both up and down, while Rothesay enjoyed 52: in winter, however, Dunoon had 14 and Rothesay only 12 (including eight by Wemyss Bay).

The Caledonian Railway, having been refused Parliamentary permission to own steamers themselves, had to form a subsidiary concern, The Caledonian Steam Packet Company, to do so. Initially with second hand tonnage and then with a fleet of steamers setting new standards of elegance undreamt of other than on the tourist boats, the new company soon turned the tables on their railway rivals. Gourock opened as a railhead on 1 June 1889 with great expectations and Dunoon at a stroke was brought eight minutes closer to Glasgow.

Was an outlay of over £600,000 worth it for eight minutes? The Caley directors certainly thought so. Apparently on 4 June the time from Glasgow to Dunoon by express train to Gourock and *Ivanhoe* was a mere sixty-five minutes, three minutes ahead of schedule. In summer a separate steamer was despatched from Gourock to the satellite pier

A very crowded *Athole*, belonging to Captain McLean, discharging at Dunoon in the 1880s. By this time the pressure on berthing space at Dunoon was intense and a new pier was becoming ever more essential

of Kirn but in winter one steamer had to cover both. It is documented that on 26 February 1890 the Sou'-West connection *Sultana* was seen steaming fast round Battery Point as the new *Caledonia* was still loading passengers from the 4.12 express train at Gourock. She was soon let go and the race was on – neck for neck for some time – but eventually the new steamer forged ahead and reached Kirn Pier first. When she eventually tied up at Dunoon the clocks indicated 5.12 pm, a mere hour from Glasgow Central Station despite the intermediate call. On 8 May, the CSP paddler *Meg Merrilies* completed the journey in 58 minutes, sailing directly from Gourock. That was hailed as the fastest on record.

Relationships between the Dunoon Commissioners and the fledgling Steam Packet Company were not always cordial. Despite all the good omens and the shortening journey times the actual number of sailings and their distribution throughout the day did not improve. In winter especially Dunoon felt aggrieved as the Caley Company refused to sanction a connection with their 5.20 pm train from Glasgow as the steamer connecting with the 4.12 train sailed on to Innellan and Rothesay and no other steamer was available. The Dunoon representatives pointed out that Rothesay already had an alternative, and faster, route via Wemyss Bay, but this argument was ignored. In summer too late evening sailings were refused except on Saturdays.

It therefore could hardly have been a surprise to the CSP when Dunoon actively supported their rivals, the Sou'-West, in their fight back. Captain James's brother, Captain Alex Williamson, had become Marine Superintendent of the G & SW fleet and brotherly love was conspicuous by its absence. Eventually obtaining Parliamentary powers to own their own steamers (with certain restrictions) the Sou'-West purchased outright the Turkish fleet and set about building three new high class fliers. These tactics certainly checked the Caley advance: perhaps even checkmated it for the time being.

The 'five o'clock racers' continued to be the most frenetic of the day and the competition has been described as acute, uncompromising and wasteful. Captain James himself would stand on Gourock Pier around 4.40 pm to urge on his fleet. Passengers at both Prince's Pier and Gourock were hustled from train to steamer so that prompt departures were adhered to. There were three steamers leaving each pier for the same destinations but the severest competition was for Dunoon. The CSP paddler usually on this station was the *Galatea* while the G & SW put the *Mercury* on the run. The Caley ship had the shortest distance to cover but the Sou'-West had the undoubted edge on speed. It was reckoned that if the G & SW boat had speeded past Battery Point before the Caley's gangway was off the betting (literally) was on her; otherwise the Caley boat would just win the race.

Not just speed but colour dominated the Clyde scene during these golden years – and an observer on Dunoon Pier would see them all in the course of a typical summer's day. Early in the morning the ships of the three railway companies would vie for the traffic for the city. The Caledonian Steam Packet steamer would have creamy all-yellow funnels, dark blue hulls and pale pink upperworks, while the Sou'-West, possibly the prettiest on the Clyde, sported red funnels with black top, with light grey hulls and white saloons; both had white, ornate paddle boxes. Perhaps less bright and fresh-looking was the North British steamer, with her red funnel with broad white band and black top, black hull and paddle boxes and cream saloons.

Just before ten o'clock would come the procession of tourist boats – the *Columba* with her bright red funnel with black top and thin black hoops, cream saloons and varnished deck house, the *Lord of the Isles* with her kenspeckle funnels, red with two narrow white bands enclosing a black one, and a black top – both had black hulls and paddle boxes – and the *Ivanhoe*, which looked like a Caley boat except that her paddle boxes were black.

Later in the day came the all-the-way older excursion steamers from the Broomielaw, owned by Captain Buchanan and looking rather dull compared with their younger sisters – hulls and paddle boxes were black and what saloons there were were white; their funnels were a sombre black with a broad white band. The same colouring was adopted by Captain John Williamson, the third brother involved in steamship management, whose *Benmore* and later also *Strathmore* kept up the old packet services from the coast to the city carrying goods probably more than passengers.

CALEDONIAN STEAMERS

JUNE SERVICE

STEAMERS LEAVE DUNOON FOR GOUROCK at (6.25, 7.40, 7.55 A.M. on Mondays), (8.0 A.M. except Mondays), 8.35, 9.40, 11.5 A M., 12.10 (1.25 P.M. on Saturdays), 2.10 (3 10 except Saturdays), 3.55, 4.10, 4.50, 5.30, 6.10, 7.10, 7.55 (8.55 P.M. on Saturdays).

TRAINS LEAVE GLASGOW (Central) FOR GOUROCK, 7.10, 8.30, 8.45, 9.0, 10.0, 11.5 A.M. 1.0 p.m (1.20 P.M. on Saturdays), 2.0 (2.30 on Saturdays), 4.12, 5.20, 7.5 (8.20, and 9 0 P.M. on Saturdays), with Steamers in connection for DUNOON, &c.

STEAMERS LEAVE DUNOON FOR ROTHESAY at 9.30, 9.45, 10.20, 11.5 A.M. 12.17 P.M. (2.15 on Saturdays), 3.20 (3.25 on Saturdays), 5.0, 6.15, 8.10 (9.35, and 10.12 P.M. on Saturdays).

ROUND THE ISLAND OF BUTE BY "GALATEA".

(DAILY EXCEPT SATURDAYS).

FROM DUNOON, 11.5 A.M.; INNELLAN, 11.20 A.M.

RETURN FARES—Saloon, 2s, Fore-Saloon, 1s 6d.

TO ARRAN (DAILY) BY THE "IVANHOE."

FROM KIRN, 10.10 A.M.; DUNOON, 10.20 A.M.

RETURN FARES—Saloon, 3s; Fore-Saloon, 2s.

CIRCULAR TOURS—STEAMER & COACHES.

FROM DUNOON at 9.40 A.M., to GOUROCK, COACH to WEMYSS BAY, and "IVANHOE" Back to DUNOON, or *vice versa.*

FROM DUNOON at 9.40 A.M. to GOUROCK, COACH to WEMYSS BAY, STEAMER to ROTHESAY, and thence to DUNOON.

FARES FOR THE ROUND, 2s.

FROM DUNOON at 10.20 A.M. by "IVANHOE," or 11.5 A.M. by "GALATEA," to ROTHESAY; Moodie & Wallace's Coaches at 11.30 A.M. and 12.30 P.M. to KILCHATTAN BAY, and Steamer from there at 2 P.M. (except Saturdays), and 4.30 P.M. on Saturdays.

FARE FOR THE ROUND, 2s 6d.

Caledonian Steam Packet Co., Limited,
302 Buchanan Street, Glasgow.

The Dunoon services of the Caledonian Steam Packet steamers of June 1894 and (overleaf) the same for the Glasgow & South Western steamers. They show the volume of river traffic using the pier at Dunoon

Cowal Heritage Trust

Glasgow & South-Western Railway Coy's.

SALOON STEAMERS.

⟶ JUNE SERVICE ⟵

Swift Saloon Steamers 'MERCURY,' 'NEPTUNE,' and 'MINERVA'
LEAVE DUNOON for PRINCES PIER at (6.35 on Mondays), 7.50 (8.25 on Mondays), 9.15, 10.25 A.M., 1.55, 3.35, 4.10 (4.55, Saturdays excepted), 5.10, 5.35 (Saturdays only, 6.10), 7.25 (Saturdays only, 8.35 P.M.).

TRAINS LEAVE GLASGOW (St. Enoch) for PRINCES PIER at 8.20 (8.30, Dunoon only), 8.55, 10.5, 11.5 A.M., 12.5 (1.5 on Saturdays), 2.3, 2.45, 4.5, (5.5, except Saturdays), 5.58 (7.40, except Saturdays) (8.3 and 9.5 P.M., Saturdays only), with Steamers in connection for DUNOON, &c.

DAILY EXCURSIONS TO THE ISLAND OF ARRAN
BY THE 'NEPTUNE.'
FROM DUNOON at 10.15 A.M.; INNELLAN at 10.30 A.M.
RETURN FARES—Saloon, 3s.; Fore-Saloon, 2s.

TO KYLES OF BUTE.
FROM DUNOON at 11.10 A.M. (3.15 P.M., Saturdays only); INNELLAN, 11.25 A.M. (3.30, Saturdays only).
RETURN FARES—Saloon, 1s 6d; Fore-Saloon, 1s.

TO ARROCHAR (LOCH LONG) FOR LOCHLOMOND,
EXCEPT SATURDAYS.
FROM DUNOON at 10.25 A.M.; KIRN, 10.30 A.M.; INNELLAN, 10.10 A.M.
Passengers have 2½ hours ashore, affording time to walk or drive to Loch Lomond (Coaches wait the Steamer's arrival. Return Fare, Arrochar & Loch Lomond, 1/-). Steamer returns from ARROCHAR at 3 P.M.
RETURN FARES—Saloon, 1s 6d; Fore-Saloon, 1s.

TO AYR, CALLING AT LARGS, FAIRLIE, AND MILLPORT,
Every MONDAY by the "Glen Rosa."
FROM KIRN at 10.15 A.M.; DUNOON at 10 25 A.M.; INNELLAN, 10.40 A.M.
Passengers have 2 hours ashore at Ayr; Returning at 3.30. P.M.
RETURN FARES TO AYR—Saloon, 2s 6d; Fore-Saloon, 1s 6d.

CIRCULAR TOUR—Steamer and Coaches (Saturdays Excepted).
FROM DUNOON at 11.10 A.M.; INNELLAN, 11.25 A.M., to ROTHESAY, thence per James M'Millan's Coaches to KILCHATTAN BAY, and thence per "Marquis of Bute" back to ROTHESAY *via* MILLPORT, FAIRLIE, and LARGS; returning from ROTHESAY at 6.45 P.M.
FARES FOR THE ROUND (including Coachman's Fee and Pier Dues), 3s 6d.

An adequate pier – at last?

With the standards and speed of the new ships on the Firth improving all the time it is not surprising that the burghers of Dunoon were beginning to feel the inadequacy of their pier. Few improvements had been made: in fact the opposite was the case. There was an outcry about the disgusting state of the waiting room and the general air of delapidation about the place. It was in 1890, following feelings of frustration, that the question of actually purchasing the pier from the Hafton Trustees began to be taken seriously once again, almost ten years after the previous attempt had ended in failure. The single berth was a distinct drawback. On the Glasgow Spring Holiday at Easter that year severe overcrowding had taken place and many complaints had been made. The pier was just too small, and the situation was not helped of course by the three rival railway companies running steamers at almost the same hours and causing further unnecessary congestion.

At the April meeting of the Commissioners a deputation was appointed to wait upon the Trustees, to lay the whole matter before them and to ask for their proposals in the circumstances. This was the beginning of a long period of discussion between the two bodies. Matters were brought forward slightly when on 7 November the two sides, together with Captain James Williamson and another Clyde master, examined the pier with a view to extension and improvement. A fortnight later soundings were taken near the Castle Rocks – but thereafter it was talk, and more talk. Eventually the Estate offered the pier and ferry rights to the burgh for £30,000 but in October 1891 a plebiscite narrowly rejected this overture as the people considered the price too high.

It was fully three years before the negotiations reached crisis level. In August 1894 the Trustees made public that they had drawn up plans and had applied to the Board of Trade for permission to build an extension to the existing pier. At their meeting on 5 November, however, the Commissioners heard the Convener of the Pier Committee report that Mr WR Copland CE, had been appointed Engineer and Mr Andrew Beveridge of London as Parliamentary Agent to try to wrestle the pier from Hafton, and that the Pier Committee desired power to lodge objections to the extension plans. The Commissioners understandbly felt that it was they who should control entry into the town and so it was agreed unanimously that this power should be given.

The stage was now set for a keen Parliamentary contest and it looked as if a great deal of bitterness would develop and a great deal of money squandered which might otherwise have been spent on a new pier. Fortunately both parties realised the folly of such a fight and a great deal of correspondence passed between them with claims and counter claims on both sides. Eventually the Trustees made a firm offer of the pier to the Commissioners for £27,000 but a seeming irrelevance was added when this price was deemed not to include the nearby Skating Rink as the Burgh representatives had wished. This offer was again rejected by the Commissioners who maintained that the rink had been included in earlier correspondence. Letters continued to go to and fro but matters had once again reached deadlock.

On the assumption that negotiations would eventually be success-ful the Commissioners had meantime arranged meetings with the steamship owners who wished to satisfy themselves about tonnage terms, how long such terms would be in operation and whether pier dues would continue to be collected.

At last, on 12 June 1895 the Pier Convener was able to intimate to a special Board meeting that the Hafton Trustees had relented and had agreed to include the Skating Rink in the purchase price of £27,000. The pier was to change hands at midnight on 31 December 1895, the end of the Trust's financial year. Approval of the terms was duly proposed and seconded. One Bailie moved as an amendment that the terms be rejected – he did not even find a seconder. At a subsequent meeting, on 20 August, the Burgh Engineer was instructed to prepare detailed plans of an extension to the pier to be submitted to the Board of Trade.

Despite the protracted nature of the bargaining both sides emerg-ed with some credit. The price paid was hardly excessive considering the pier was a going concern and not a mere structure. The Hunters of Hafton had erected the pier at their own risk and had had a fair amount of expenditure because of storm damage over the years: the Trustees quite rightly had had to protect their own interests during the negotia-tions. On the other hand, the Pier Committee, ably supported by the Burgh Commissioners, had protected the interests of the community by their skilful bargaining. They had obtained for £27,000 a business for which the sellers had first demanded £35,000 and had completed the transfer of the pier to the burgh without any recourse to law.

The pier duly changed hands at the appointed hour. Bunting stretched across the entrance and as midnight struck on Hogmanay 1895

The North British Steam Packet Company's *Lucy Ashton* as she was when she celebrated the transfer of Dunoon Pier to the Burgh on New Year's Day 1895

cannons were fired in the Castle grounds. Next morning at 8 o'clock when the NB steamer *Lucy Ashton* left the pier for Craigendoran rockets were let off from her deck.

It was not long before controversy arose. The Burgh Commissioners had to borrow an exhorbitant £40,000 to buy the pier and extend it and there was considerable debate about whether the extension should be to the north or to the south. Final agreement to start was given on 14 January 1896 and soundings for the foundations of the new piles commenced within a fortnight. A strong letter from the Steamship Association, representing many of the masters of the Clyde paddlers, effectively put paid to any extension north towards Kirn as the authors gave very cogent reasons against such an action. Incidentally Kirn Pier renovations also started in the same month.

The Burgh Pier Committee agreed at their meeting of 7 February to give the contract for the works to James Watson of Glasgow who was to be given £14,539/12/6 (£14 539.63) for his pains and he was to be allowed fourteen months to complete the job. Work started in earnest at the beginning of March and within days the Esplanade had been barricaded in, rock had been blasted, the railings on the parapet in front of the castle removed and large quantities of contractor's plant landed by sea. A local contractor, Alex Melville, was unanimously appointed Inspector of Works at a salary of £3 per week. It was reported that one of the applicants for the job had been "considered steady" but this was during the interview changed to "takes a hauf."

The new pier at Dunoon was described in the local press as follows:

"The works in connection with the new Pier include a sea-wall some 300 yards long, to be formed of rubble concrete, which will be surmounted by an iron railing of ornamental design. The pierhead will be 440 feet long by 60 feet wide; the gangway, forming connection with the centre of the pierhead, being 170 feet long and 40 feet wide.

"The structure will be entirely of timber, secured together by iron bolts and sheathed in places with iron plating. The piles, carrying-bolts, pierhead, and gangway are 12 inches in section, the pierhead being formed of six rows of piles, shod with iron shoes, and varying from 50 feet long in front to 40 feet long at the back. All timber-work exposed to the action of the sea is greenheart, the fenders and coping being of American rock elm, and the flooring of pitch pine, creosoted to guard against decay.

"The front, back, and end piles of the pierhead will have a batter of 1 in 16. The hand-rail on each side of the gangway will be 3 feet 6 inches in height. At low tide the depth of water will be 10 feet, and at high tide 20 feet."

Rather more colloquially one correspondent stated: "The new Pier looks braw on paper, but it means a big braw price."

In April a temporary wooden stage was erected to facilitate piling operations, about 450 piles being required. A huge cargo of cement was landed and a large steam crane erected while a powerful steam hammer was put in place to drive the piles into the river bed. The first pile was to be driven on 19 May but at the crucial moment the jib of the steam crane broke and the socket, jib and pile plunged into the water, crashing through the woodwork – fortunately without injury. It was therefore not until Wednesday 20 May 1896 that the first pile was put in place by the daughter of Mr William Maton, the Piermaster. Ten days later fifteen piles had been secured.

The next six weeks saw frenzied activity. By mid-June the new gangway being erected south of the existing one had almost reached the line of the old quay and the building of the breast wall was well advanced. One labourer was badly injured one morning when he was climbing the scaffolding with a barrow. The jib of the crane came round and the bucket attached to it struck him and threw him to the ground. The bulletin from the hospital declared that "he was as well as could be expected."

And then on 1 July all operations ceased. The party line was that this was "to obviate any interference with steamboat traffic." It is true that July saw the busiest traffic on the firth and that the works were beginning to interfere with the increased numbers boarding and disembarking from the steady flow of steamers. But there was another reason for the work coming to a sudden halt.

Such an operation needed Parliamentary approval and this had not yet been granted. Application had been made through the proper

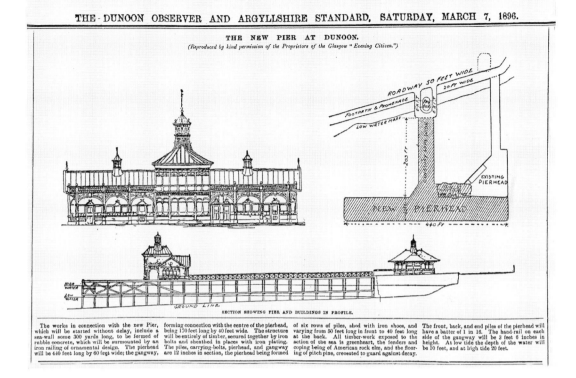

THE DUNOON OBSERVER AND ARGYLLSHIRE STANDARD, SATURDAY, MARCH 7, 1896.

THE NEW PIER AT DUNOON.

(Reproduced by kind permission of the Proprietors of the Glasgow " Evening Citizen.")

SECTION SHOWING PIER AND BUILDINGS IN PROFILE.

The works in connection with the new Pier, which will be started without delay, include a sea-wall some 300 yards long, to be formed of rubble concrete, which will be surmounted by an iron railing of ornamental design. The pierhead will be 440 feet long by 60 feet wide; the gangway, forming connection with the centre of the pierhead, being 170 feet long by 40 feet wide. The structure will be entirely of timber, secured together by iron bolts and sheathed in places with iron plating. The piles, carrying-bolts, pierhead, and gangway are 12 inches in section, the pierhead being formed of six rows of piles, shod with iron shoes, and varying from 50 feet long in front to 40 feet long at the back. All timber-work exposed to the action of the sea is greenheart, the fenders and coping being of American rock elm, and the flooring of pitch pine, creosoted to guard against decay. The front, back, and end piles of the pierhead will have a batter of 1 in 16. The hand-rail on each side of the gangway will be 3 feet 6 inches in height. At low tide the depth of the water will be 10 feet, and at high tide 20 feet.

channels and on 2 June the Provisional Order Bill under the General Pier & Harbour Act of 1861 duly passed its first reading in the Commons. Unfortunately history appeared to be repeating itself and just as the original purchase from the Hafton Trustees was dogged by seeming irrelevancies like the sale of a skating rink so the Provisional Order was linked to a similar petition from Helensburgh for a similar pier extension. While the steamship owners did not object to the Dunoon application they opposed the clauses relevant to Helensburgh and so the Bill could not proceed. It took some weeks to persuade the G & SW Railway, the main opposition, to give way but eventually success came. It was not, however, till early August that the Bill finally passed into Law.

Piling resumed, then, in August but progress for a while was slow. By now the new gangway was some sixty feet farther out to sea than the original structure. Because it was jutting out some steamers had difficulty in berthing at the old pier while on leaving they had to go astern a fair distance before the master could ring Full Ahead. The *Columba* allegedly was barely able to berth at all and David MacBrayne stated that he would withdraw her calls and instruct her to sail direct from Kirn to Innellan if any further piling were carried out. The commissioners had to ignore this threat if their plans were to be adhered to and, from 17 August, the 300 foot paddler duly bypassed the pier.

That Monday morning, with no notice in the *Glasgow Herald*, passengers were on Dunoon Pier awaiting her arrival when word reached them that the boycott was on: spring traps sped them together with the northbound mails to Kirn Pier and they managed to board the great paddler just in time. It was indeed galling to see the Clyde's second longest vessel, the palatial Arran steamer *Glen Sannox*, call on a special excursion for Ayr Junior Conservative Party en route to Garelochhead only two days later. Apparently she was never within fifteen feet of the new structure. MacBrayne's motives were really called into question in September when the smaller *Iona* took over the Royal Route and still bypassed the pier although she had called twice daily in summer while sailing on her own roster.

The work speeded up in September after the second last row of piles of the new gangway were in place. The extension south some 220 feet was then started and the full distance was covered by early November. The workforce was augmented and all that remained was to drive in the outer row of piles, surface the structure and join the old and new piers. This progress was despite several setbacks. In late August a worker was thrown into the water while he was preparing to hoist a pile from a floating raft. Sunday 30 August was the night of a severe summer storm when waves crashed over the new pier, drove pontoons ashore and carried away some contractor's plant while on 8 October there was an exceptionally high tide which caused both old and new piers to be under water.

For the second time work suddenly stopped – on 12 December. The workmen were paid off and returned to Glasgow. £6000 had been spent but much remained to be done. On Boxing Day (there were no Christmas holidays in these days) the Commissioners issued Watson with an ultimatum – return to work within seven days or lose the contract. The tactic paid off, for on 4 January work recommenced with twelve labourers and a carpenter employed to drive the single row of piles to link the old and new piers. No legal action was contemplated. Throughout March, despite the suspension of labour during frequent gales, work proceeded apace and the men sometimes worked early and late in the day to suit the tides. Meanwhile the Commissioners gave a Kirn joiner, James Drummond, the contract to build within three months a pier Waiting Room and Pay Box at a cost of £2963. The existing offices at the end of the old pier gangway were then able to be removed. A temporary gangway was also erected alongside the new gangway so that the work could be expedited and, so that shelter would be available for the seasonal traffic, temporary waiting rooms and a pay box were constructed.

A new berth

At last the south berth was ready for opening. It was hanselled early on Monday 31 May 1897 by Captain John Williamson's new steamer *Strathmore* which that season brought over the morning papers from Gourock before making for Rothesay and her main run of the day up to Glasgow. The old entrance was now barred and the old pier reserved purely for goods traffic.

All steamers now called at the southern extension and so Dunoon remained for the time being a single berth pier. This allowed the old pier to be extended out some sixty feet to the level of the new and by early August the piling was all but completed except for the row intended to repair the north face of the pier where the goods steamers berthed.

Williamson's *Strathmore* which opened the South Berth on 31 May 1897

The cross bracing and deck planking came next. The Commissioners then decided to imitate Tighnabruaich Pier which was the only one on the firth with electric light. On 21 August twenty one electric lights, either incandescent or arc lamps, were switched on and created "an exceedingly brilliant effect". A month later the good burghers or Dunoon were able to gaze upon "waiting rooms with their balconies and minarets unequalled in the west coast for artistic design and gorgeous display". Now back in favour, James Watson and his men were treated to a special excursion to Inveraray with a sail on the *Fairy Queen* on Loch Eck and lunch on the *Lord of the Isles* after boarding at Strachur.

A difficulty arose in September, a month of severe weather when progress was slow. At a special meeting of the Dunoon Commissioners it was agreed that a signal box above the new waiting room, as on the original plan, would be too exposed and a signal cabin should be erected elsewhere. Mr Copland, the Engineer, was sent away to devise a new plan and he duly came back with a £200 scheme for the signal box, to include a fog bell, to be put up just to the south of the new gangway. A decision was delayed until a meeting on the pier in December produced agreement. Meanwhile the renovations to the original pier were completed and by November Dunoon at last became a two berth pier. The local press concluded that this merely encouraged racing. The Calvinistic Commissioners at the same time decided to dispense with a Refreshment Room and replace it with an office for the pier clerks.

1897 ended in near disaster for the pier. A severe gale removed the temporary pay box when the sea broke over it as the storm was at its height. Six weeks later a real gale and strong sea caused huge waves to lash over the abutment on which the new pier offices stood, throwing heavy spray across the pier entrance. In the late afternoon of 12 February the Esplanade and pier offices were completely enveloped in spray. The sea carried away most of the guttering and smashed a pane of plate glass when water poured into the south entrance.

To compound the problems a dispute arose between the contractor and the engineer and for the third time labour was withdrawn. Solicitors representing Watson alleged in a letter to the Commissioners that the contract had been completed and that repairs to the old pier were in fact outwith any agreement. The Pier Committee in reply gave the contractor seven days' notice to remove his plant and materials. They also instructed their engineer to employ men to complete the repairs to the north end of the old pier. Agreement was reached also to purchase furniture for the waiting room from Wylie & Lochhead and A Gardner & Co of Glasgow, to accept an offer to erect a four-dialled clock guaranteed against steamers thumping into the pier, to buy a horse from Chalmers of Greenock for £42, to experiment with turnstiles and to buy a 5 ton crane for the discharge of goods. They agreed to delay

The new Dunoon pier in the early stages of building; early 1897

Dunoon Pier as it was during construction: August 1897

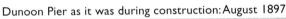

An M&L National Series postcard of the turnstile building: circa 1900

THE PIER, DUNOON

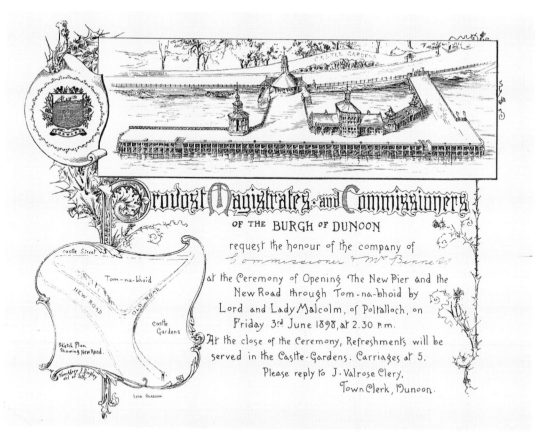

One of 350 official invitations to the Official Opening of the Pier on 3 June 1898.
Unfortunately the great day was marred by torrential rain

placing the crane until the strength of the pier was tested. Apparently no one had considered the need for a crane in the plans and the decking had not been reinforced to withstand its weight.

By May everything was complete. The pay box and luggage accommodation had been finished at the entrance while on the pierhead now stood the first and third class waiting rooms and the ladies' retiring room, together with the pier offices with the piermaster's room above. The walls were wooden in the form of "Swiss shingling" while the roofs were covered with red tiles. A goods store in the same style had been completed at the north end of the pier so as to be convenient to the cargo steamers' berth. Meanwhile the Engineer, Mr Copland, entertained the Commissioners to dinner – in the pier waiting room. It was suggested by one of the august body that Piermaster Maton should wear a frock coat with brass buttons stamped with the burgh crest. As these would cost 65/-, the motion was declined.

Ceremony in the rain

Three hundred and fifty invitations were sent out for the official Opening Ceremony on Friday 3 June 1898. Local schools and businesses were given a holiday. At half past two that afternoon Lord and Lady Malcolm of Poltalloch landed right on schedule from their steam yacht *Lutra* at the steps behind the new signal box. They then proceeded via the waiting room to the shore end of the new gangway. Bailie Anderson of the Pier Committee then asked Lady Malcolm to cut the ribbon placed across the pier entrance and she duly obliged. The two chief guests were invited on to an improvised platform to meet the Provost of the day, Provost Doig. Speeches ensued and Lady Malcolm was presented with a golden key to mark the ceremony before the invited guests made their way to the Castle Gardens for refreshments.

Unfortunately the proceedings were marred by torrential rain throughout. Umbrellas were everywhere and the dignataries were dressed in oilskins and waterproof boots. Nevertheless Dunoon was *en fête* and the burghers were understandably jubilant that their "truly elaborate pile" had been successfully completed, despite its formidable cost. Just as the VIPs were leaving the pier the *Columba* called in on her run to the Broomielaw. Cannons were duly fired in celebration.

The various steamer companies must have taken full advantage of the new facilites because by the end of the year Dunoon Pier received a thousand more calls than in 1897.

Meanwhile a letter had appeared in the local paper urging the Pier Committee to charge a penny for the use of the lavatory in the first class waiting room. Some "obviously third class passengers" had been using it.

The worst storm for many years hit the Clyde on 27 December 1898. The gale was from the south west and was accompanied by torrential rain. During high water in the afternoon the waves broke clean over the gangway and the south side of the pay office and the nearby breast wall were damaged by the heavy seas. Despite the extra cost the Pier Committee decided to erect a new breast wall which would deflect the sea from the paybox in a future storm but it was well into the spring before repairs were completed.

The *Kenilworth* (left) and *Caledonia* at the pier: early 1900s

The last piece of equipment for the pier had arrived – the turnstiles. They were soon fixed into their positions and opened for business on 5 June 1899. The new Dunoon Pier was now complete in all aspects.

During the whole process of negotiation and construction there were not a few incidents at Dunoon. In the summer of 1893 the CSP's *Galatea* and Buchanan's veteran *Vivid* were both racing for the pier. There was no contest as far as speed was concerned but the old boat had had a head start and in fact was signalled to take the berth. Nothing daunted, Captain Bell of the Caley boat ignored the signal and slipped in ahead. The inevitable fine followed.

The frustration of the single berth was made acutely clear about lunchtime one sunny August day in 1896 when the NB's new flier *Talisman* broke down when a damper jammed as she was coming alongside the pier. She was on the down run to Rothesay and her passengers were transferred to the G & SW's *Marquis of Bute* but until she resumed service some time later she obstructed the pier completely and any passengers from another vessel wishing to disembark had to clamber over her decks to get ashore.

The *Talisman* was involved in an incident just a month later when she was in a *contre-temps* with one of the Sou'West's crack ships, the *Neptune*. About 300 yards off the pier the two collided and the paddle box of the North British vessel was slightly damaged. In the *mêlée* the Caley's *Marchioness of Bute*, having approached from Gourock, cheekily slipped in and took the berth.

The *Talisman* was involved in yet another incident in June 1898. She had left Dunoon on the 7.55 am run to Craigendoran and was making all speed for Kilcreggan Pier. The *Chancellor* from Prince's Pier was racing for Kilcreggan also and, although by the rules of the sea she should have slowed down when she saw the NB boat to starboard, she kept on and the two vessels collided. Neither master was contrite, however, because the two ships started to race once again until the

Talisman eventually took the pier first. Later her captain, John Gray, was presented with a marble clock by some passengers "in recognition of the ability displayed in handling the ship by which serious loss of life was averted." There was precious little objectivity in Clyde steamer racing.

A letter to the paper concluded that:

> "racing between the coast steamers has become so prevalent as to be looked upon almost as part of the normal routine. The crew has got so accustomed to it that they get no more excited over a spurt than they do in heaving luggage about."

Even ships of the same company vied with each other. In July 1897 the *Duchess of Rothesay*, the CSP's latest new addition, and the *Ivanhoe*, just taken over by the Caley, raced hell for leather between Innellan and Dunoon. Perhaps surprisingly, the *Rothesay* only won by a single length. On such occasions, of course, there were always extenuating circumstances to excuse the poor performance – overcrowding, poor coal, barnacles on the hull, etc.

Gales could damage not only pier buildings but also steamers. The storm of 30 December 1897 caused the tugboat which carried the early mails to sail straight from Kirn to Rothesay but Captain Munro of the Caley's *Marchioness of Breadalbane* was more foolhardy. On the 7.15 am run from Rothesay to Gourock he had to slow his engines two or three times on passage. While approaching Dunoon his ship encountered the full strength of the up-river swell and the forward bulwark, port paddle box and stern were quite badly damaged while he took the pier. Worse, the mate was pinned by the force of the sea against the engine room grating and was severely injured. Her master impervious to the danger, the *Breadalbane* returned to Dunoon for her scheduled call at 9.40 and did more damage, both to herself and the pier. When she left for Gourock she almost collided with the *Talisman*, which was lying off. Three steamers made no attempt to call but MacBrayne's winter boat *Grenadier*, after several attempts lasting about half an hour, managed to tie up. On her departure she was loudly cheered.

An incident which had its funny side took place in July 1898. Yet another new North British paddler, the *Kenilworth*, was on the up run from Dunoon to Craigendoran at lunchtime when a rope caught one of the seamen and he was flung into the water. Fortunately he was a strong swimmer and had no difficulty in reaching the shore. The *Kenilworth* did not wait for him but headed off at all speed for Kirn Pier to take it before Buchanan's *Isle of Bute*. She did not in fact make

John A Stirling collection

The statue of Dunoon's Highland Mary on Castle Hill above the pier.
The statue, in memory of Mary Campbell, was unveiled on 1 August 1896,
the year work started on the present day pier

it but the upshot was that the poor seaman, soaked to the skin, had to wander aimlessly round Dunoon for a couple of hours till his ship reappeared en route to Rothesay in the afternoon.

There were, however, more significant happenings around Dunoon Pier in the 1890s. Not strictly relevant to the pier but appearing in many photographs of it is the statue of Highland Mary. It was unveiled by Lady Kelvin on 1 August 1896. No one thought at the time of the significance of the next event, although it was to change the face of the Clyde and its fleet of steamers in later years. On 24 February 1898 two motor cars were landed at the pier, it is believed from Williamson's *Benmore*, in the afternoon. They were for the Glasgow & West of Scotland Motor Company and were to run between Dunoon and Sandbank on the Holy Loch. Built in Coventry, they could carry eight passengers and attracted a great deal of attention. On their trial run the next day they took 25 minutes to reach their destination. The first car actually went into service on 4 March.

If, however, one had asked a reader of Scotland's national dailies in the late nineties what made Dunoon newsworthy it would be none of the above. Dunoon became notorious throughout the land for its reaction to the Sunday Breakers.

The paddle steamer *Victoria* which was at the centre of the Sabbatarian controversy at Dunoon pier in 1897.

The Sunday Breaker

Scotland was very much a Sabbatarian country in the nineteenth century and the influence of Calvinism was widely felt, especially in the Highlands and Islands. In 1853 a steamboat called the *Emperor* had attempted to break the ban on Sunday sailings and had fallen foul of more than one pier proprietor. That very year the so-called Forbes-Mackenzie Act was passed – it allowed publicans to sell liquors on Sunday but only "for the accommodation of lodgers and *bona fide* travellers."

Gradually more shady characters got in on the act and realised that money could be made by buying an old steamer and running it from Glasgow on the Sabbath. One of the most disreputable was Harry Sharp, a Gallowgate publican. The river steamers were outwith the jurisdiction of the Act and at any rate it could be claimed that passengers on board were 'Boney Feedy' travellers. Fortunately for Dunoon, Sharp and others did not attempt to disturb the peace of the Sabbath by attempting a landing. Greenock and Rothesay were the favourite destinations – not that it mattered to those on board as they were in no fit state to remember anything of where they had been. During the eighties legislation was passed which stopped the sale of alcohol on board a steamer on Sunday if she was returning to port the same evening, and from 1883 there were no Sunday boats on the river, as there was no longer any profit in it.

It was in February 1897 that the people of Dunoon first received word of a steamer possibly bringing travellers to their pier on a Sunday. The ministers of the town were vehemently opposed to the suggestion and asked their parishioners to sign a memorial condemning such a move out of hand. 1701 did and the Commissioners almost unanimously took their part. Letters appeared in the local paper, the majority from the more liberal townsfolk who stated well-rehearsed anti-Sabbatarian views. One writer, signing himself 'X', reckoned that the petitioners had "scared the Commissioners out of their wits and that they, in the most silly fashion, [had] succumbed to the united forces of teetotalism and superstition in the name of Religion."

Another correspondent, 'Alpha', talked about unmitigated cant and reckoned that Dunoon was fast becoming "the headquarters in the Highlands of religious lunacy."

The vessel at the centre of the storm was the *Victoria*, a fine two-funnelled paddler which had originally been the douce flagship of the old Wemyss Bay fleet but, apart from a brief interlude sailing to Campbeltown, had since been employed down south. She arrived in the Clyde from the Thames on 23 April and immediately was sent for overhaul in Glasgow. She emerged with yellow funnels and black top, finely fitted out, commanded by Captain Kerr and managed for the Clyde Steamers Ltd by Mr Andrew D Reid. Her first voyages were on Saturday 8 and Sunday 9 May. On the Saturday she sailed, via Dunoon, to Rothesay and round Bute and Cumbraes and was advertised to sail at 10 o'clock on the Sunday morning to the same destinations. Tickets were valid for return by the G & SW steamers the following day and no strong liquor or drunks were to be allowed on board.

By the appointed hour that peaceful sunny Sabbath morning the Broomielaw was packed with thousands of spectators. The Commander-in-Chief of the Salvation forces in Scotland had positioned choristers at the gangway to sing sacred songs like: "Out upon Life's ocean sailing, Heading for another sho-o-ore."

Some would-be travellers were conscience-stricken and turned back but four hundred went on board for a highly enjoyable outing. The *Victoria* left a few minutes before ten amid cheers and much waving of handkerchiefs. On board were men, old and young, with "a fair sprinkling of young ladies."

About twelve o'clock she reached Prince's Pier, which was packed throughout its whole length with curious spectators. 36 went on board, including a nun, Sister Veronica, who had travelled overnight from her convent in London, having been summoned by telegram to attend an urgent case in Dunoon. As the Sunday breaker approached Dunoon those on board realised that there were dense crowds behind the pier gates to see the fun. About a hundred yards off the steamer blew her whistle twice for the pier signal but there was of course no response as there was no one on the pier. There was quite a strong wind and, despite the cheering of the crowd gathered round the new statue of Highland Mary, the *Victoria* found taking the pier impossible as there was no one to take her ropes. Eventually Andrew Reid, on the bridge, shouted that they were not going to use the ship's boats to get ashore and would-be visitors to Dunoon were to record their names on a paper in the cabin as a form of protest. The ship sailed on to Rothesay (and a tumultuous welcome) to the strains of "The Lost Chord" and Mozart's "Twelfth Mass" (in English).

On the return voyage leaving Rothesay about six in the evening, Sister Veronica pleaded with the master and the chairman of the Company, appropriately called Major Ferry, to put her ashore at Dunoon and voiced her astonishment at what she perceived to be the narrow-mindedness of the Scottish people. The eventual agreement of Captain Kerr brought renewed cheers from the passengers. As the *Victoria* neared Dunoon, with the pier gates still barred, everyone came on deck and soon realised that there were some 3000 people on land giving the appearance of Glasgow Fair Saturday rather than Communion Sunday. It was a tricky approach as the new berth was not quite ready and of course projected beyond the old structure.

Eventually the steamer was near enough for two of the seamen to jump ashore. Soon they were able to pull in the ropes accompanied by tremendous cheering from ship and shore. As the gangways had been carefully stowed away the 22 passengers, including the nun, had to leap ashore.

Getting off the steamer was one thing: getting off the pier was quite another. The gates were locked and guarded by police. Only one passenger was agile enough to climb the railings and pass over the new breast wall. The others tried begging the police to let them through but to no avail. Even the cries of Sister Veronica were not heeded. They even asked the police to arrest them and take them to the Police Station but that did not work either as they were already considered to be prisoners. The deadlock continued for the best part of an hour and the denunciation of the Commissioners who had closed the pier became louder and louder. Eventually the situation was saved by one of the Commissioners themselves who managed to enter the pier through a window in the waiting room and open the inner gate. He tried to unlock the large gate but it would not budge. Instead he escorted the beleaguered travellers through the window by which he himself had entered. The police just looked on. As they paraded up the main street they were followed by crowds of people applauding them and urging them on. Later Sister Veronica pronounced the whole episode a ludicrous farce and added that if had not been for her habit she would have scaled the fence without any compunction. She had seen too much of the world to be put off entering the town in such a way. Provost Cooper was quite unrepentant. Newspapers from the *Partick Star* to the *Manchester Guardian* lambasted the Dunoon Commissioners, declaring that all they had done was to give free advertising to the "nefarious promoters" and to heighten the feeling against "rigid and unreasoning Sabbatarianism".

The following Sunday the *Victoria* was once again advertised to call at Dunoon en route to Rothesay but intending passengers were warned that they might not be able to leave the pier, in which case their tickets would be valid for Rothesay. In the event, the steamer, now with 700 on board, did call at the goods berth down the side of the old pier but despite a formal altercation between one of their leaders, Mr Graeme Hunter, and the Police Superintendent guarding the gates, no attempt was made to force an exit. The whole question of the legality of the Commissioners' ban was to be debated at the Board of Trade soon afterwards and the steamboat company did not wish to prejudice the case.

Sunday 23 May saw the Victoria bypass Dunoon completely. In fact she struck a log coming down the river and broke a paddle float. Temporary repairs at Renfrew allowed her to reach Rothesay two hours late. On the last Sunday of the month she passed Dunoon and cheekily dipped her flag in salute.

A poem appeared in the *Sketch:*

> Dunoon, Dunoon! beware of the day
> When the anti-Sabbaoths shall claim thee as prey,
> And passenger steamers o' Sundays shall glide
> With "wicked" excursionists far down the Clyde;
> Proud Provost, beware! bold Bailies, take heed!
> Nay, lay up thy claymore and rein in the steed.
> For one day excursionists boldly will land
> And play on your Pier with a jubilant band,
> And thus having battled and lost at the game,
> The doughty Dunooners will welcome the same.

The very day that the *Strathmore* opened the new south berth at the pier Vice-Admiral Sir George Nares, of the Board of Trade, conducted an inquiry in Dunoon Burgh Hall into the now notorious By-Law No 5 of the Dunoon Commissioners:

A rowing boat from the *Victoria* similar to those transporting the 'Boney Feedy'
travellers ashore during a Sunday sailing

The episode of the Sunday Breakers at the pier attained folkloric status in
Dunoon. Seventy years later the episode was re-enacted (below) during the
Dunoon Pageant

Dunoon Observer

"No steamer or other vessel shall be permitted to land or embark passengers at the pier between 12 midnight on Saturdays and 12 midnight on Sundays without the special sanction of the Commissioners, under a penalty by the party or parties in charge of said steamer or other vessel of a sum not exceeding £5 for each passenger landed or embarked in contravention thereof."

The counsel for the Clyde Steamers Ltd, owners of the *Victoria*, made great play of the fact that in the Statute creating Dunoon Pier it was stated that at all times there should be free access. Sir George appeared impatient with the Commissioners' advocate's insisting on giving the arguments for the creation of the By-Law in the first place and eventually terminated the inquiry, refusing permission for the Sabbatarians to give evidence. His judgment in due course was eagerly awaited.

Meanwhile the *Victoria* called at the new south pier quite amicably during the week. The following Wednesday the band played "See, the conquering hero comes" as she was warped into her berth while the next day, ironically, she burst a steam pipe while alongside and was forced to remain at the old pier during repairs which lasted until the Friday evening. On Sunday 6 June, however, Mr Graeme Hunter, the *agent provocateur* of the previous encounter, arranged for passengers to be ferried ashore at the Castle rocks. Five thousand gathered to watch a fair number disembarking – including six ladies bodily carried ashore by the ferryman. This procedure was followed each Sunday for some weeks, to the delight of the Dunoon townsfolk.

It was not long, however, till trouble flared up again at Dunoon – on a tropical Glasgow Fair Sunday. It had been announced in advance that from then on passengers from the Sunday-breaker would disembark at the pier and not by ferry. The boat was crammed from stem to stern and some ten thousand gathered round the pier gates at Dunoon to join the fray. The day being very calm, the *Victoria* berthed at Dunoon with ease. Mr Hunter, wearing knickerbockers and a Norfolk coat, was first off to catch the ropes. Over a hundred passengers then jumped from the paddle box and marched up the pier to demand that the gates be opened. The request was of course refused.

What followed could easily have become rather ugly as policemen were bodily removed from their positions by the supporting crowd while the strong men among the passengers stormed the gates, which, being temporary, yielded fairly quickly, and gained their freedom. In the evening the Piermaster had the good sense to unlock the gates and allow the dense crowd on to the pier: the cheering was heard by the worshippers in the nearby parish church. An enterprising restaurateur had dared to open his shop in the Pier Road during the fun and did a roaring trade. Meanwhile the *Pall Mall Gazette* hailed the breaking of the Dunoon Pier gates as an epoch-making event – "a manifestation of the irresistible might of the popular will" against the Commissioners whose place was "in some museum of antiquities."

The Board of Trade decision came a few days later and determined the next moves. The Board allowed and confirmed the By Law with the express purpose of allowing it to be tested in a Court of Law. The steamboat company, knowing that they faced a fine of £5 per passenger landed, arranged for three gentlemen to disembark the next Sunday and confront the Police Superintendent at the gates. They were not allowed through and so returned to the steamer to find that small boats were alongside ferrying the passengers ashore. While this was going on the crowds outside broke down the gate to the old pier and quickly gained access to the new. Steamer passengers mingled and easily went ashore. Included in the crowd were the three gentlemen.

The Dunoon Commissioners thus had a *prima facie* case for prosecuting the captain of the *Victoria* and claiming £15 from the Company – they were urged to press their case immediately. Two days later a meeting of the Pier Committee supported that view by a single vote but the full council declined to support them. Having doggedly refused to give in on their deeply held Sabbatarian principles they threw in the sponge just when they could have won a legal victory. In so doing they forfeited the goodwill of the clergy and other Sunday observers while at the same time exposing themselves to ridicule throughout the whole country.

Sunday 1 August saw a new tactic from the *Victoria* – she landed her passengers at Kirn Pier, a mile north of Dunoon, without any trouble. Extra police had been drafted in to Dunoon and the crowd of 6000 were more than a little disappointed at missing the fun. During the month passengers were landed and picked up either by ferry at the Castle rocks or at Kirn Pier, but on Sunday 22 near disaster struck. A strong westerly was blowing and when the *Victoria* stopped engines off the Castle rocks she gradually drifted out so that the boats had the best part of a quarter of a mile to row. Passengers were disembarking from the lee of the steamer, unseen by those on the shore, when one of the boats capsized and several passengers were thrown into the water, one being in serious danger of drowning. Fortunately there was no loss of life but the incident put an end to the lighthearted atmosphere which had prevailed on previous Sundays. Caution reigned in the following weeks and nothing unremarkable happened during September or until the *Victoria's* last voyage on 10 October.

It was reported in June 1898 that Mr AD Reid had two former Clyde steamers fitting out at Kelvinhaugh in Glasgow. One was the *Victoria* but the second was none other than the old NB flier *Jeanie*

Deans. In fact the *Victoria* was soon sold and once again left the Clyde for the South Coast; the *Jeanie Deans* was renamed *Duchess of York*. A new company had been registered to operate her – the Glasgow Steamers Ltd.

The new *Duchess* made her début on Sunday 19 June. She was advertised to sail from the Broomielaw to Greenock, Dunoon and Rothesay. One plus point was that AD Reid had enticed the famous Brescian Family to play music on board and this attracted the crowds. Dunoon was lined with spectators but they were to be disappointed. After sailing within a hundred yards of the pier the steamer turned away sharply and continued her voyage to Rothesay passing outside the Gantocks. In fact she made no attempt on subsequent Sundays to call at Dunoon and even sailed close to the Renfrewshire coast on her way down firth.

Then the Commissioners played into the hands of the Sunday breakers. On Saturday 2 July the CSP paddler *Meg Merrilies* had a special excursion from the coast to Gourock with train connection to Glasgow for Barnum & Bailey's "Greatest Show on Earth". On the return journey the *Meg* was due to reach Dunoon just before midnight but as the train was running late it was actually twenty past twelve before she tied up at the pier. No objection was made to this call which quite clearly contravened By Law No 5. Reid immediately ordered his secretary to send a letter to Piermaster Maton asking if, now that the pier was open on Sundays, there was an extra charge for catching the ropes. The following Sunday the same problem arose but despite this the Commissioners did not budge and refused to allow the unwanted vessel in. The decision was not challenged and in fact the company ceased trading at the end of the season.

The *Duchess of York* was offered for sale in the summer of 1900;. AD Reid must have obtained some backing because the old paddler was reboiled during the following winter and reappeared in 1901 under the banner of Messrs Reid Ltd. 1900 had seen a further interloper in the Sunday trade. The old Arran steamer *Heather Bell*, which had sailed on the Clyde in the early seventies, came back to fill the gap and gained a certain notoriety by attempting on three successive Sundays in July to land passengers at Dunoon. She was unsuccessful and was subsequently sold to North Wales.

Reid obviously decided that he would force a showdown with the Dunoon Commissioners in 1901. The rejuvenated *Duchess of York* commenced sailing at the end of May and included Dunoon in her Sunday itinerary. On 30 June she succeeded in attracting about eighty passengers, including women and children, to defy the ban on Sunday sailings at Dunoon by offering a through booking to Ardnadam on the Holy Loch by connecting coach and an optional coach drive to Loch

Buchanan's *Isle of Arran,* seen here leaving Dunoon, was a great rival of the *Duchess of York* for Sunday sailiings during 1902

Eck. Barricades and barbed wire were erected by the Council but the steamer carried ladders which the crew placed in position so that passengers could avoid the obstacles. Although police were on duty and the usual large crowds assembled the passengers were orderly and no arrests were made. The constabulary did not try to prevent passengers from entering or leaving the pier, despite criticism from the Sabbatarian lobby.

The steamer continued to call all summer and eventually the Commissioners realised they had to take legal advice with a view to either suing the owners of the *Duchess of York* or seeking interdict against them. This they did but to their chagrin the opinion of counsel, made public on 16 December, was that they had no legal right to prohibit passengers landing at the Burgh Pier on Sundays. Early in 1902 the By Law was finally repealed.

The result was that the pier was open to all comers and the *Duchess of York* had to fight off competition from the Buchanan steamers *Isle of Arran* and *Isle of Bute* which entered the fray in June and sailed on alternate Sundays. Originally advertised to leave the city at 11am the time was soon put back quarter of an hour to avoid clashing with the start of church services. The Buchanan boats made such a success of Sunday sailings that eventually, in 1909, the Caledonian Steam Packet Company decided to take the revolutionary step of introducing their own first ever Sunday steamer on 6 June. Despite strong opposition, the *Duchess of Hamilton* sailed from Gourock to Dunoon and Rothesay. The Caley fleet grew in popularity and often the steamer was filled to capacity from Rothesay alone.

The pioneer turbine steamer *King Edward* approaches Dunoon: in the early 1900s

The Caledonian's *Duchess of Fife* keeps ahead of the Sou'-West *Mercury* as they race from Dunoon (seen in the background) to Innellan: ca 1905.
By 1903, Dunoon passengers could be disembarking a mere 49 minutes after leaving Glasgow Central

Children playing on the beach in West Bay watch the *Minerva* pull away from the pier: ca 1900. In Glasgow Fair week 1907 passenger returns at Dunoon reached 100,000 for the first time. Six years later the figure for the week was 123,215

A new century

During the twelve years from the initial defiance of the Sunday-breaking *Victoria* to the respectable railway steamers' joining the contest much had happened on the wider scene. The closing years of the nineteenth century witnessed the resurgence of the North British fleet. With new ships like the *Talisman, Kenilworth* and ultimately the *Waverley*, NB honour was restored and the Company were able to scoop up a fair amount of traffic which the south bank rivals had previously won over. The Craigendoran route became very popular with the commuters from Dunoon and the fast connection by train to Edinburgh (Waverley) was an added bonus.

The administration of Dunoon was altered by the Town Councils (Scotland) Act, which declared that from 31 December 1900, "a Town Council shall be elected by every Burgh . . . and shall be designated by the corporate name of the Provost, Magistrates and Councillors of the Burgh." It was Councillors rather than Commissioners who now decided the fate of Dunoon Pier, but the faces were the same as the same public-spirited burghers continued in office.

The death of Queen Victoria in 1901 was the end of an era in many ways, not least in the field of marine engineering, with the Clyde the proving ground. A remarkable set of circumstances had caused a new ship to be launched which in its own way was almost as revolutionary as the pioneer steamboat *Comet* nearly a century before. This was the *King Edward* – a very appropriate name heralding a new age. She was the world's first commercial turbine steamer, using a novel method of propulsion (much more efficient than the old reciprocating engine) which drove her, with remarkable economy of fuel, at over 20 knots. Not only was she fast, she was also smooth and silent. On 28 June 1901 the white-funnelled steamer, operated by Captain John Williamson of the *Strathmore*, made her first call at Dunoon Pier to uplift VIPs for a special cruise to Campbeltown. During the voyage she sailed past the Caley flagship *Duchess of Hamilton* with consummate ease. Three days later she took her place on the long day trip to Campbeltown, the Clyde's most farflung destination. She attained instant popularity, so much so that the following year the same builders, Denny's of Dumbarton, produced a bigger and at almost 22 knots even faster turbine steamer to be her consort, appositely named *Queen Alexandra*. Her maiden voyage brought her to Dunoon on the very day that the signing at Vereeniging heralded the end of the Boer War, 2 June 1902. All the Clyde steamers were dressed overall and in the course of the day the new "Queen" fired saluting shots in celebration.

Meanwhile the railway companies were replacing some of their ageing vessels. Most prominent among the new batch, introduced in June 1903, was the Caley's *Duchess of Fife*, as graceful as any ship on the river. She was placed on the midday run to the Kyles of Bute, a roster which incorporated the five o'clock race for Dunoon, and the new paddler was able to give the Sou'West's *Mercury* a run for her money. Dunoon passengers could now be disembarking a mere 49 minutes after leaving Glasgow Central.

Sadly William Maton, piermaster since before the building of the new pier, had died in service in January of that year and so did not witness the new exciting twist to the railway rivalry. He was succeeded by Archie Ferguson, who was appointed Interim Piermaster until 13 October, when his post was made substantive.

The introduction of the turbine, the new tonnage of the three railway companies and the increasing popularity of Sunday sailings all combined to boost the receipts at the turnstiles to Dunoon Pier. Yet another factor was added, the introduction of the massive purification works which were designed to remove the foul odour of the River Clyde in Glasgow. As a result the All-the-Way sailings from the Broomielaw received a major boost and new tonnage was built for the Buchanan and Williamson fleets to cope with the upsurge in traffic.

On Glasgow Fair Monday 1902 Dunoon Pier had an amazing 104 steamer calls. In Glasgow Fair Week 1907 passenger returns reached six figures for the first time while in the corresponding week six years later an astonishing 123,215 streamed off the pier. These increases were recorded despite the pooling agreements between the south bank railway companies whereby from 1909 the most wasteful competition was diminished; certain routes were given exclusively to one company and steamers not required for the slimmed down services were laid up.

In order to increase the amenity for passengers at Dunoon Pier a wooden screen with a glass top was erected the full length of the passenger gangway early in 1910. The great storm of November 1912 did damage the pier, but perhaps not as much as some other quays on the Clyde. The goods shed and gangway suffered most.

As well as the Clyde river steamers and the cargo vessels a further type of vessel occasionally called at Dunoon. This was the cross-channel ship. An outing to Ireland would be advertised and one of the Laird ships would call at Dunoon early in the morning, around half past six, to take passengers on board for a day trip to Portrush. Originally

The Glasgow & South Western Railway's *Neptune* at the south berth: ca 1900

employing the *Rose*, the Company soon found that the newer and larger *Hazel* was needed to cope with the ever-increasing traffic. The river steamers themselves in addition to their daytime schedules would be advertised for evening cruises to many of the resorts of the Clyde, not just the main ones like Rothesay, Millport or Brodick but also to the quieter watering places like Kilchattan Bay. Non-landing cruises up the lochs, through the Kyles or to the Arran coast were also popular.

Most steamers at that time featured a band which played all the repertoire of the day – Viennese waltzes, Victorian and Edwardian parlour songs and Gilbert and Sullivan melodies. While some excursions were advertised by the companies others took place under charter and many local organisations used the evening cruise, or occasionally a full day cruise, for publicity, reward or fundraising. Prominent among charterers was the Glasgow Cowal Society, whose annual trips on one of the foremost steamers was one of the highlights of the year for Dunoon and the villages from Blairmore to Innellan.

This period at the start of the twentieth century was not entirely without incident, especially in heavy weather. During a 1905 storm, when, uncharacteristically , the CSP steamers did not attempt to take the pier, MacBrayne's *Grenadier* did and shattered her port paddlebox in the process. The following June, the CSP's *Duchess of Hamilton*, now for the first time on a cruise roster in the Upper Firth, was leaving Dunoon for an afternoon trip to Loch Goil when she was run into by the G & SW Kyles steamer *Neptune* arriving from Prince's Pier. Late 1909 saw the Sou'West's winter boat *Mars* attempt the pier from the south because of wind and swell. She eventually berthed and a gangway put on board. Passengers in twos and threes managed to get ashore when a rope snapped and the gangway was dragged into the water. It was immediately crushed by the paddlebox against the pier and the steamer had to abandon her call and make for Greenock leaving intending travellers behind.

A crowded *Isle of Cumbrae* alongside at
Dunoon: ca 1910. World War 1 saw a big
reduction in this kind of traffic as vessels were
requisitioned, some never to return. During
the war years this ship became a ferry
between Greenock and Dunoon

The Great War and after

The Great War started in Europe on 4 August 1914. The Clyde season was in full swing and few changes were noticed immediately. The first came on the 27th of the month when the Dunoon authorities warned that the pier lights were liable to be extinguished without further notice. It was on 1 July 1915 than an anti-submarine boom was put in place between a point just south of Dunoon Pier and the Cloch Lighthouse. The Clyde services were partitioned and anyone travelling from Dunoon to Rothesay now had to travel by road to Innellan and catch the steamer from Wemyss Bay. A month later, at the request of the Admiralty, the four separate companies carrying goods to the coast from Glasgow were brought together under one concern, Clyde Cargo Steamers Ltd, so that a minimum service could be provided.

That summer Dunoon was still served by six railway steamers from the three railheads together with six excursion steamers from Glasgow, but in 1916 the number of each was halved. In that year too all railway Sunday sailings ceased, although the Buchanan boats lasted until Easter of the following year. Paddle steamers, with their shallow draft, made successful minesweepers and most of the more modern ships were soon to be requisitioned for service under the white ensign, some never to return. The *Lord of the Isles* kept sailing from Glasgow to Dunoon and Lochgoilhead but by 1917 she was the only pleasure steamer left. The three railway companies, under a joint Shipping Controller, largely had to make do with chartered tonnage and veterans from the MacBrayne West Highland fleet appeared on Clyde services. The most usual vessels at Dunoon in the darkest days of the war were the *Isle of Cumbrae*, *Ivanhoe* and *Dandie Dinmont*. Ancient vessels like the *Glencoe* (1846) and the *Gael* (1867) were to be found relieving the cargo vessels from time to time. The civil population of Dunoon were suffering the privations and hardships of war in common with the rest of the nation.

The war days were not without exciting incidents at the pier. During a September gale in 1917 the *Chevalier*, which had been on the run from Gourock on charter to the CSP since July, did not cant away from the pier quickly enough and went aground in shallow water.

In fact she heeled over rather alarmingly as waves lashed her decks with spray. The few passengers on board were taken ashore soaked to the skin in a small boat. Four months later the captain of the *Isle of Cumbrae*, on the final Sou'West run to Dunoon and the Holy Loch, misjudged his approach in the dark and caused his ship to smash heavily into the pier. The steamer sustained a fair amount of damage to her rails, paddlebox and paddlewheel and did not resume her chartered sailings till mid-April.

Armstice Day was 11 November 1918 but it was many months before Dunoon and the Clyde services returned to anything even approaching normality. Restrictions on through services to Rothesay were removed on 1 February of the following year and the boom itself was quickly dismantled. Only MacBrayne's *Chevalier* took advantage of this. It was another three months before the railway steamers gave through Dunoon-Rothesay sailings.

Several ships which had survived the war had not returned from Admiralty service, or were in dock being modernised, and so chartering was still the order of the day. Despite that the Clyde managed fairly well in 1919. Railway fleet operations were still controlled by the Government and to a large extent the various units operated under one umbrella; certainly one timetable was issued for all three companies.

Meanwhile Dunoon's piermaster Archie Ferguson resigned on 22 April 1919 when he received a position in Harrogate. He was succeeded by Mr Dugald Cameron, who had previously been a member of the Town Council.

Travellers from Dunoon must have thought that wartime austerity had returned during the spring of 1921. That was the time of the miners' strike which caused such an acute shortage of coal. Steamers were laid up through lack of fuel and Dunoon had to make do with calls from one steamer of each of the three railway companies, together with MacBrayne's, each day.

MacBrayne's veteran *Glencoe* on duty on the Clyde

Fleet amalgamations

G iven the circumstances of the day the Railways Act of 1921 was inevitable. Larger units of management were necessary and so the original railway companies were grouped on a geographical basis, the Caledonian and Glasgow & South Western both coming under the aegis of the London Midland and Scottish Railway and the North British becoming part of the London & North Eastern Railway. The use of the word 'London' at the start of each title was significant. Scottish railways were from 1923 under London control. No obvious difference was to be seen in the north bank fleet but on the south bank the new grouping did bring about fairly obvious and far-reaching changes.

To the man in the street the most striking was the changed liveries of the steamers. Funnels were repainted, the bottom two-thirds being basically Caley yellow and the top third Sou'West red with black top. The Caley *Duchess of Fife* actually had her funnel repainted while she was lying at Dunoon Pier. The so-called 'tartan lums' were very unpopular and only lasted two years, plain yellow funnels with black top superseding them.

The 'five o'clock race' for Dunoon was a thing of the past. The pattern which emerged was that at 5 pm the steamers for the coast left from Prince's Pier with a connection from Glasgow (St Enoch) while an hour later there was a connection from Glasgow (Central) via Gourock. The colour had gone but so had the wasteful competition.

The Clyde had actually witnessed an amalgamation of steamer companies four years previously. The up-river fleets of Buchanan Steamers and Captain John Williamson came together in 1919 as Williamson-Buchanan Steamers Ltd. All steamers adopted the white and black funnel and, together with the turbines of similar livery, the combined fleet now contained eight steamers. This provided formidable competition to the railway companies. The two turbines, the *King Edward* and a second *Queen Alexandra*, had the day excursion trade to Campbeltown and Inveraray sewn up while the paddlers, by the time they reached Dunoon from the Broomielaw, were ideally placed to capture the lucrative afternoon excursion traffic. In addition their fairly new paddle steamer *Queen-Empress* gave a variety of day cruises from the coast resorts taking advantage of a niche in the railway boats' schedules which could not be filled because of war losses. The pre-war procession of day cruise steamers departing from Dunoon between nine and ten in the morning was completed, as before, by MacBrayne's *Columba* but also by two of the LMS fleet – the Caley turbine *Duchess of Argyll* which now sailed to Arran via the Kyles and the former G & SW paddler *Jupiter* which was placed on a variety of long day trips. Sadly some of the fliers on the Rothesay station survived the war but were shadows of their former selves. The *Mercury, Talisman* and *Kenilworth*, for example, were not the sleek racers they used to be.

One aspect of life which did return to normal during 1923 was the restart of the Sunday service given by the CSP/LMS from Gourock. Williamson-Buchanan had already recommenced as early as 1920 but it was a further eight years before the LNER followed suit and introduced a service from Craigendoran. Apparently Dunoon pier tolls were double the normal price for Sunday arrivals and departures. As Sunday evening departures from Dunoon became more and more popular the beginning of the end for the special early Monday morning departures was heralded. No longer did a dozen steamers converge on the three upper firth railheads every Monday packed with weekenders returning to the city.

Monday 25 November 1925 was uncharacteristically calm on the firth. The cargo steamer *Lapwing* was discharging at the front of Dunoon Pier when the weight of a furniture van on her crane made her heel over at a dangerous angle. Suddenly the jib of the crane snapped under the strain and the van struck the ship's gunwale as it fell. This accentuated the list, caused some cargo to shift and allowed water to pour in through open scuttles. In the nick of time, just as she was starting to sink, the *Duchess of Fife*, lying at the other berth, got ropes aboard and towed her into shallow water at the north of the pier. There she settled and was actually completely submerged at high water. The *Lapwing* was carrying livestock at the time but fortunately, apart from one horse, the animals all managed to swim ashore and were saved. The ship herself was eventually raised and reconditioned. When she reappeared the next year her name had been changed to *Cowal*.

The post-war industrial unrest which had been fomenting since 1919 and 1921 culminated in the General Strike of 1926. As far as transport was concerned the crucial groups to withdraw their labour were the railway workers and the miners. At the end of May the railway service to Dunoon was provided by only three steamers, two LMS and one LNER, supplemented slightly by the white funnelled fleet and the *Columba*. The high costs of repairs, the prohibitive price and scarcity of coal and the shortage of materials in general meant that when the strike was finally over its repercussions continued throughout the season. Railway and steamer fares rose and the services were less

Dunoon Pier about 3.30 pm with *Mercury* at the berth and the *Duchess of Rothesay* arriving, both in their tricolour funnels: 1923

Buchanan's *Isle of Arran* (foreground) and Williamson's *Benmore* before amalgamation: ca 1900

Clyde Cargo Steamer *Cowal*, formerly the *Lapwing*, after her mishap at Dunoon: late 1920s

LONDON MIDLAND AND SCOTTISH RAILWAY AND CALEDONIAN STEAM PACKET COMPANY

STEAMER EXCURSIONS and CRUISES

from

DUNOON AND KIRN

AUGUST, 1926

DATE	PARTICULARS OF SAILINGS	LEAVING AT		RETURN FARES	
		Dunoon	Kirn	Cabin	Steerage
Daily ..	To ARRAN, via Kyles of Bute, returning via Garroch Head, by Turbine Steamer " Duchess of Argyll " or other Steamer	a.m. 9 30	a.m. 9 22	s. d. 4 6	s. d. 3 0
Daily ..	KILCHATTAN BAY TOUR (Steamer and Coach) : Steamer to Kilchattan Bay, thence Coach to Rothesay, returning by Steamer	9 30	9 22	3 9	—
Daily except Saturdays ..	To the KYLES OF BUTE and ORMIDALE (Loch Ridden) by Steamers " Duchess of Fife "	11 10	11 5	3 0	2 3
Saturdays ..	and " Jupiter "	p.m. 3 10	p.m. 3 5		
Mondays, Wednesdays and Fridays	The ROUND of the LOCHS and the FIRTH of CLYDE by Steamer " Jupiter " or other Steamer. Cruise includes the Round of the Islands of Bute and Cumbrae, Kyles of Bute, Loch Ridden, Loch Striven, Loch Goil and Loch Long ..	a.m. 9 25	—	5 3	3 9
*Tuesdays and Thursdays	To AYR by Steamer " Jupiter " or other Steamer	9 25	—	4 6	3 0
Mondays, Wednesdays and Fridays	AFTERNOON CRUISE to LOCH GOIL and LOCH LONG, by Steamer " Jupiter " or other Steamer	p.m. 2 30	—	3 0	2 3
By P.S. "JUNO"					
Monday, 23rd	To GARELOCHHEAD.. ..	12 55	—	2 7½	2 7½
Thursday, 26th	To LOCHGOILHEAD	12 55	—	2 7½	2 2½
* Will not sail on Thursday, 5th August.					
By Steamers "DUCHESS OF ARGYLL" or "JUPITER"					
Sunday, 8th	ROTHESAY and FALLEN ROCKS (Arran)	12 20	—	3 0	—
Sunday, 15th	ROTHESAY and LOCHRANZA (Arran)	12 20	—	3 0	—
Sunday, 22nd	ROTHESAY and SKATE IS-LAND (Loch Fyne)	12 20	—	3 0	—
Sunday, 29th	ROTHESAY and BRODICK BAY (Arran)	12 20	—	3 0	—

CONDITIONS OF ISSUE OF EXCURSION TICKETS.

Excursion Tickets are not transferable, and will be available only to and from the Stations or Piers named upon them and by the Trains or Steamers and on the dates specified on the announcements.

The Company give notice that Tickets for Excursions are issued at a reduced rate, and subject to the condition that the Company shall not be liable for any loss, damage, injury or delay to Passengers arising from any cause whatsoever.

DONALD A. MATHESON,
Deputy General Manager (for Scotland).

GLASGOW, *August*, 1926.

H. G. BURGESS, *General Manager.*

The London Midland and Scottish Railway/Caledonian Steam Packet Company programme of sailings from Dunoon: August 1926. The repercussions of the General Strike meant that what was on offer was much more spartan than usual

The West Bay Kiosk and the revolutionary turbine steamer *King George V*: early 1930s. Apart from her novel machinery and other original features, she was the first Clyde steamer to have her promenade deck enclosed amidships with large observation windows

The white-funnelled *Queen Alexandra* (with enclosed promenade deck) and the LNER's new *Jeanie Deans* at Dunoon: ca 1935

frequent and the operation less efficient. It was a far cry from thirty years before when glorious railway competition was at its height and the Dunoon folk were still celebrating the acquisition of their pier from the Hafton Estate.

Matters would have to improve and, despite the 1929 Wall Street Crash which brought the Depression to Europe, they eventually did. One spin off was the increasing number of English holidaymakers who arrived in August as they found Scotland a cheaper alternative to holidays abroad. Meanwhile the Dunoon Women Citizens' Association urged the Town Council to remove the seats at the end of the pier "as people sit and spit and give a bad impression to visitors entering the town."

The very year of the General Strike produced the revolutionary

A dramatic shot of the twin red funnels of the
great *Columba*: August 1934

white-funnelled turbine *King George V*, which, apart from her novel machinery and other original features, was the first Clyde steamer to have her promenade deck enclosed amidships with large observation windows. She called twice daily at Dunoon from September that year en route to Campbeltown or Inveraray. Then three years later the LMS took the brave decision to build a turbine fairly closely resembling the 1926 vessel and to use her specifically as a one class ship (first of course) for cruising. When the *Duchess of Montrose* appeared in 1930 she became enormously popular, so much so that in a sense she spawned a further series of celebrated vessels – her sister ship *Duchess of Hamilton*, the paddle steamer *Jeanie Deans* for the opposition LNER, and the pride of the 'doon the watter' fleet the turbine *Queen Mary*.

By the end of the thirties not only had the top of the market cruising fleet been renewed but also the ferry class paddlers. In fact only three steamers built in the nineteenth century remained in active service. Of course the delight in welcoming newcomers was always tinged with sadness at the departure of the old faithfuls, none more so than on 18 September 1935 when the great *Columba* sailed on the Royal Route for the last time. Her departure from Dunoon at 4.10 pm that day was scarcely marked but everyone was aware that a precious link with the past had gone for ever.

MacBrayne's *Columba* approaching Dunoon for
the last time: 18 September 1935

The pier rejuvenated

During all of this expansion and renovation of shipping, Dunoon Pier itself underwent a very welcome facelift. By 1934 the annual number of calls at the pier topped the eleven thousand mark for the first time. On Easter Saturday of that year Dunoon scored a first on the Clyde Coast. In response to the increased traffic and to facilitate passenger control a loud speaker system was installed in the signal tower and announcements of the various vessels' berths and destinations were given. Between announcements traditional Scottish accordion music was played on gramophone records.

This innovation was small fry, however, compared with the alterations set in train by Dunoon Town Council at their January meeting in 1937. They agreed to spend £3000 and sanctioned the erection of a pier shelter. The structure was to be 220 feet long and 20 feet broad with a four foot canopy in front of the existing building extended southwards. Provision was made for a tearoom and a new signalling tower at the south end together with a new screen on the passenger gangway. The front of the shelter was to be eight foot high rising to twelve feet at the rear. The burgh architect was to prepare a contract but apparently he took ill and neglected to have the plans approved by the Dean of Guild Court before work started. Although the Department of Transport had approved the plan it was still illegal. Despite the fuss generated locally the plans nevertheless went through the Court retrospectively without amendment.

Further ill will was caused when the pier staff had to vacate their office during construction work but more seriously it was soon discovered that the basic structure underneath the proposed new tearoom was requiring a fair amount of remedial work and strengthening. The renovations received a further setback on 30 April when a worker's blow lamp used to burn off old paint started a fire which claimed a large section of the woodwork of the waiting room at the head of the gangway. The

troubles were soon forgotten, however, when on the day of the Coronation of King George VI on 12 May well over five thousand jubilant holidaymakers streamed through the turnstiles giving the Council's coffers a considerable boost.

Perhaps it was the general goodwill surrounding this great national occasion which prompted the Councillors to amend their original plans, spend more money and incorporate a promenade within the design. The piermaster's office was to be moved to allow a stairway to be constructed to the balcony. They also allowed personal weighing machines to be installed in the ladies' toilet. By midsummer it was realised that the shelter was inadequate and agreement was reached that it should be extended northwards by some 54 feet. The signal tower was reconstructed on top of the balcony at its south end and during the winter an additional stair was put in place underneath.

The improvements proved very acceptable and many flocked to promenade on the pier balcony. Later dues were charged for the privilege. The tearoom flourished, the piermaster now had a new office at balcony level and a little information kiosk was even added on the esplanade to provide a much-needed service. Dunoon once again led the way among the coast resorts.

Sadly Dunoon seemed to have more than its fair share of accidents. Potentially the most serious had occurred on 1 October 1930. The old *Caledonia* was making for the pier on her evening commuter run when without warning she scraped her bottom along the Gantock rocks. She quickly developed a considerable list but fortunately this was soon righted and her master was able to berth her at the pier and disembark the 400 passengers who were aboard. Although there had been a light on the Gantocks since 1886 apparently the glare from the shoreline made the buoys on the rocks difficult to make out. Captain Brown retained his job but the LMS had to pay out £3000 in repair costs. Ironically, just a fortnight previously a huge crowd had turned out at the pier to see the formal inauguration ceremony when Dunoon's street lighting was switched on for the first time. Perhaps the Dunoon Electricity Company had done too efficient a job.

Evening cruises of the 1930s advertised in these bills – by 1934 the annual number of calls at Dunoon pier topped 11,000 for the first time

75

A March 1939 picture of the rejuvenated Dunoon pier with the *Marchioness of Lorne* (left) and the *Jeanie Deans* (with grey hull). In January 1937 Dunoon Town Council had agreed to spend £3000 and sanctioned the erection of a pier shelter. The structure was to be 220 feet long and 20 feet broad with a four foot canopy in front of the existing building. Improvements included a tearoom, a new signalling tower and a new screen on the passenger gangway

In September 1934 the small turbine steamer *Atalanta*, a relatively unusual visitor, split the pier open to a depth of eight feet, while in March 1938 a further collision caused even more damage. On that occasion, the paddle steamer *Mercucy* was approaching the south end on the 7.30 am up run to Gourock when she swung round in a sudden gust of wind and crashed head on into the pier to a depth of some fifteen feet, sending deck planking flying into the air. The new generation of paddlers, of which the 1934 *Mercury* was one, had higher superstructure than their predecessors and this made them more difficult to handle at piers. The helmsman did not stand a chance. £1000 of damage was caused to the pier and, following repairs to a badly buckled bow, the steamer had a bar keel fitted in the hope that her performance could be improved.

The relationship between pier owner and steamer operator was not always smooth. Early in 1937 a deputation of steamer and rail season ticket holders appeared at a Council Meeting. They were daily travellers Monday to Saturday from Dunoon to Glasgow and naturally

A picture taken from the new balcony of the *Juno* and the *King Edward* approaching: on a Saturday afternoon between 1937 and 1939

the smooth running of their travel arrangements was very important for their peace of mind. Having by now taken over the Williamson-Buchanan white-funnelled paddle steamers, the LMS had put on the vital morning and evening computer runs from 21 January the rather sedate 'summer butterfly' *Queen-Empress* whch could not be relied upon always to berth at Gourock in time for the fast connecting train to the city. In fact she only did so, allegedly, under the most favourable weather conditions. Offices were not being reached by the nine o'clock deadline and tempers were being frayed. The commuters informed the Council that if they did not achieve a satisfactory resolution of the problem with the LMS they would leave Dunoon and return to live on the other side of the firth. It was the Council's turn to send a deputation to the LMS. This they did and the *Queen-Empress* was soon replaced by the much more acceptable *Duchess of Rothesay*.

One of the designs
for a possible LMS/
CSP car ferry: 1939

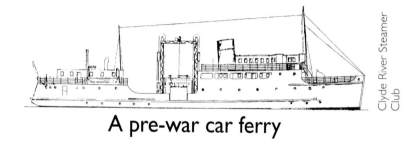

Clyde River Steamer
Club

A pre-war car ferry

It was of Dunoon that the Greenock MP Robert Gibson was thinking when he posed the question to the Minister of Transport in the House of Commons early in 1939, "Could the LMS make any improvements in the transportation of cars across the Firth of Clyde?"

Around a thousand cars were carried annually between Gourock and Dunoon in the late thirties. They could only be transported at certain states of the tide and drivers had to steer along two wooden planks in order to board. Once on the ship the cars would be stored in the vicinity of the funnel(s), the modern LMS paddlers having been built with ample deck space partly with vehicle transport in mind. Barrowloads of passengers' luggage in advance (PLA), cargoes and other goods were likewise loaded and unloaded via planks. The matter was remitted to the LMS Steam Vessels sub-Committee to investigate. The LMS were keen to grab the initiative in case a private operator jumped in and claimed the traffic.

There were car ferries in existence in other parts of Britain at the time and the CSP, as the Scottish steamboat subsidiary of the LMS, no doubt took the experience of other operators into account. A report was submitted in February and it was noted that the provision of ferry slips at Gourock and Hunter's Quay (more sheltered than Dunoon) would cost at least £33,000 while a suitable ship incorporating a lift would cost a further £35,000. A new ship was not seen as a replacement for one of the old, coal-burning paddlers but as a genuine addition to the fleet. In fact when tenders were eventually submitted for a Gourock-Dunoon car ferry the cheapest was £51,000.

Costs were of paramount importance and the Steamboat Committee had several designs to choose from incorporating a whole range of possibilities from a sophisticated car and passenger vessel to a basic car ferry. The £51,000 tender was for a 300 ton 12 knot steamer with covered accommodation for 400 passengers and a complement of 20 cars. Lifting gear, rather like the elevating platform on the vehicular ferries operating on the Clyde at Glasgow, would be incorporated forwards. As events turned out, the outbreak of war against Germany on 3 September 1939 put paid to these ideas, and a lot else besides.

The Cloch-Dunoon boom to prevent enemy shipping entering the Clyde during the Second World War

A new World War

This time round the effect was immediate. The Cloch-Dunoon boom was closed within days of the outbreak of hostilities and once again the Clyde services were divided in two. Again, unlike during the Great War, almost all the paddle steamers were requisitioned by the Admiralty within the first month of the conflict, but now there were a substantial number of turbines to take care of the coast services. The services to Dunoon from Gourock – Princes Pier was closed in March 1940 – were maintained intitially by four of the turbines in turn. On 21 October 1941 the *King Edward* was rostered for the first run from Gourock to Dunoon but shortly after leaving the railhead she collided with the Irish vessel *Lairdsburn* and was in fact subsequently employed as a troop tender.

The rôle of Dunoon ferry was eventually entrusted to the *Queen Mary II*, her name having been changed on the advent of the great Cunarder – not only her name but also the colour of her funnel which had been painted yellow and black from December 1939 to show that the Williamson-Buchanan fleet had been taken over by the CSP at

A wartime picture of *Queen Mary II* leaving Dunoon. During the war years she provided the regular ferry service. Because of blackout regulations Dunoon pier was closed during hours of darkness

Gourock. The *Mary* had previously taken the only wartime service from Glasgow to Dunoon on Easter Monday 1940. By the time she became the regular Dunoon ferry her superstructure and funnels had been painted a dull ochre but after the 1941 season all ships were to be seen only in naval grey. The quality of the paint being poor, rust quickly showed through.

The passage across the firth was tortuous as the Tail of the Bank was the world's safest anchorage for the Allies and the number of ships at anchor, from little auxiliary vessels to giant liners like the *Queen Mary* herself, was vast. Navigation was tricky and this was compounded by blackout regulations which caused many ships' windows to be boarded up so that lights could burn freely inside but not be seen externally by enemy aircraft. Dunoon Pier was also closed during hours of darkness for similar reasons and Hunter's Quay used as the alternative port for the Cowal district.

The *Queen Mary II's* commodious accommodation was often used to the full. While the English holiday market dried up, hotels were requisitioned for the war effort and the movement of naval personnel escalated beyond all expection. After the Clydebank and Greenock Blitz

Dunoon pier with the cargo boat *Marie* (far left, goods berth), *Lucy Ashton*
and *Marchioness of Graham*

in March and May 1941 Dunoon became a greater evacuation centre
than ever.

Goods traffic increased in proportion and many a barrow was
loaded aboard the turbine for the twenty minute journey across the
firth. This did nothing for the steamer's wooden decks although the
situation was eased from May 1943 when Passengers' Luggage in
Advance was no longer allowed. Livestock continued to be carried
across. One day in May 1941 a bullock attempted to bridge the gap
between the pier and the *Queen Mary II* by jumping but the poor animal
misjudged its distance and fell into the water. A lieutenant who
witnessed the scene quickly grabbed a motor boat, succeeded in getting
a rope round its neck and dragged it ashore.

Two paddle steamers still called at Dunoon – the *Marchioness of
Lorne* on the Holy Loch run from Gourock made occasional sorties
during the day and often took the sparse Sunday sailings which still
operated while the veteran *Lucy Ashton* – the same steamer as had fired
her cannon to celebrate the takeover of Dunoon Pier by the burgh
almost fifty years before – alone and virtually unaided maintained the
LNER service from Craigendoran throughout the six dark years.

Pier dues ticket book

Joseph Beatty, a stickler for discipline,
became piermaster in 1945 and served
continuously until his retirement in 1972

Just as in the First, so in the Second World War, Dunoon lost a
fine Piermaster when Dugald Cameron died in February 1940. His
replacement out of eighty applications was local man James R Watson.
It is recorded that after a local dance during his term of office there
was 'some disorder' on the pier among Naval Liberty men who were
boarding their ships. The piermaster tried to control the situation but
the liberty men merely accused him of behaving like an Admiral. The
Admiralty soon issued an apology and paid for the damage done. Jimmy
Watson did not hold office for long and following his departure the well-
known purser of the *Duchess of Montrose*, Joseph H Beatty was
appointed from seventy applicants.

The question of pier dues was constantly to the fore. Servicemen
and women were exempt but relatives of those returning on leave
complained that because of the uncertainty of the arrival time of the
steamers they had to go down the pier several times and were charged
dues each time. Joe Beatty, however, was a stickler for discipline and
correctness and it is very unlikely that he granted any favours.
Incidentally, one way pontage at Dunoon was introduced in March
1940. Instead of paying a penny each way, 2d (almost 1p) on entering
became the order of the day.

Retrenchment and nationalisation

VE Day was on 8 May 1945. Within a few weeks the boom was dismantled and through services between Dunoon and Rothesay were restored during the summer, by the *Duchess of Argyll* and *Lucy Ashton*. Once again war losses meant a diminished fleet but the LMS difficulties were compounded by the fact that all six of their steamers which did not return to peacetime service were paddlers and so there was a decided imbalance in favour of the turbines, which had limited use. Despite the very efficient point-to-point service between Gourock and Dunoon (and other ports) which had occurred during 1939-45 the management insisted on returning to the old style rosters with virtually light running and criss-crossing of the firth and the use of many satellite piers. These factors, together with the lack of decent quality coal, resulted in inefficiency and late running, while rampant post-war inflation caused financial headaches to the railway operators as fares and charges did not increase at a corresponding rate.

Unbelievably, the timetable between Dunoon and Gourock in 1946 showed sailings at a reduced frequency; so much so that the LMS put on two small motor vessels, the *Ashton* and *Leven*, as a supplementary service between the two piers. As they were slow and of very limited capacity they did not offer much relief. By 1948 an even smaller vessel, inappropriately called the *Wee Cumbrae*, was on the service on her own but after the following season it petered out. By the simple expedient of routing the Craigendoran steamers via Gourock the number of crossings to the south bank railhead was markedly increased. Around this time too the historic ferry link between Dunoon and Cloch Point was broken for ever. At least the pier itself was given a new lease of life with substantial repairs taking place.

The 'great days' of the thirties were gone for ever, although there were some excursion services. The two 'Duchesses', *Montrose* and *Hamilton* sailed down firth every day to Campbeltown, Arran or Inveraray while the *Duchess of Argyll* and a redesigned *Jeanie Deans* plied to the Kyles of Bute. All the Way sailings were restored but now only two vessels, the turbines *King Edward* and *Queen Mary II*, operated them, and the Royal Route was re-established from Gourock rather than Glasgow or Wemyss Bay. Five paddle steamers maintained the rest of the railway connection network as regards Dunoon. On 16 June 1947 an event took place which was to have great significance – the LNER reopened their sailings to Lochgoilhead and Arrochar by their new paddle steamer replacing a gallant steamer sunk at Dunkirk, the *Waverley*.

The aftermath of the Great War brought the amalgamation of the smaller railway companies; the aftermath of the Second World War brought the amalgamation of these larger units under one nationalised concern – the British Transport Commission, or, to the man in the street, British Railways. The immediate consequence was the disppearance of the distinctive red, white and black funnel of the Craigendoran fleet and its replacement by the ubiquitous buff and black, but many more fundamental changes were taking place in the background. Coordination of services started in winter and by 1950/51 the *Talisman*, a revolutionary diesel-electric paddler from the LNER stable, was on the combined service to Dunoon and Rothesay from Craigendoran and Gourock. Unfortunately she did not have the speed or reliability to maintain the published roster and the regular commuters and others became more and more vociferous in their complaints, dubbing her "the slow boat to China".

Although more expensive to operate, the faster *Waverley* was eventually substituted, but not for long. On 2 March 1951, in pea-soup fog, she hit a submerged rock off the Cowal shore while on the 8 o'clock down run from Gourock. Despite the pumps working at full power, the tearoom was partially flooded and the fire brigade had to be called out to assist after she managed to berth at the pier. While the *Waverley* was withdrawn for repairs she was replaced in turn by the even larger and more expensive *Jeanie Deans*, but she too only lasted a week before an engine failure delayed her crucial morning departure from Dunoon by two hours.

Actually the *Waverley* was not the first post-nationalisation casualty at Dunoon. In April 1949 the bow of the *Marchioness of Lorne* had penetrated the pier by some seven feet following a machinery mishap.

All was not of course doom and gloom. In the immediate post-war years Dunoon was immensely popular as a resort and this was reflected in the turnstile receipts which were even higher than during the war. With greater flexibility in the deployment of vessels pre-war excursions could be revived. Dunoon folk could once again sail Round the Lochs, Round Bute or go on a variety of afternoon cruises. But there was one new traffic problem. In the old days special services were offered early on Saturday afternoons to cater for the emptying of offices and places of work at lunchtime. With the introduction of the five-day working week, however, this flow now peaked on Saturday mornings

BTC-owned *Talisman* (with yellow funnel)
arriving at Dunoon: June 1950. A diesel-
electric paddler, she ran the combined service
to Dunoon and Rothesay from Craigendoran
and Gourock. Unfortunately she did not have
the speed or reliability to maintain the
published roster and was dubbed "the slow
boat to China"

and many relief sailings had to operate. One of the Duchesses or a large
capacity paddler was always on hand mid-morning to help out at
Dunoon while in one season the Bridge Wharf steamers were actually
rostered to double back to Gourock after calling at Dunoon and before
proceeding to Rothesay so that they could take capacity crowds to both
resorts.

The traffic from the city at holiday periods continued unabated.
On Easter Monday of 1949 Dunoon was exceptionally busy. When the
winter Ardrishaig mailboat *Lochfyne* called on her return journey she
could only take a further sixty aboard. The *Jupiter* on her ten to six
run to Gourock left 500 while the *Duchess of Hamilton* an hour later
could not accommodate everyone as the queue numbered more than
2000. Eventually she returned for an extra sailing and cleared the pier.

A fine shot of the *Duchess of Montrose* leaving
the south berth: 1947

A car ferry at last

An event of the greatest significance for Dunoon and the other resorts on the Clyde occurred in 1950 – the derationing of petrol. Prior to that event almost everyone travelled on holiday or on day trips by rail. Now the door was open for a boom in the use of the private motor car which heralded the eventual demise of the train as the mode of transport for the English tourists or the Glasgow day excursionists. It became even more urgent that the new nationalised concern address the question of car transport across the firth, shelved in 1939 by the advent of war.

Two other factors supported this strategy. On 31 October 1949, despite the intervention of Major McCallum, MP for Argyll, Dunoon received its last call by a cargo steamer. From that date on goods were transported by road – by British Road Services from Glasgow. There were still cargo boats on the Clyde, now owned and operated by the Railway Executive, but they bypassed Dunoon and the other mainland resorts and concentrated on the islands alone. Any dual-purpose vessel which could handle cargo as well as cars and passengers would be an economically sound investment and allow the antiquated vessels to be withdrawn.

The other consideration was similar. The use of the satellite piers like the Holy Loch piers, Hunter's Quay, Kirn and Innellan was becoming less and less relevant as road transport advanced. In the past the quickest and most convenient way of getting to Dunoon from the smaller townships in Cowal was by steamer but now with the greater use of buses and lorries a steamer journey seemed less appropriate. Remembering the efficient point-to-point service during the war, the Scottish Region of British Railways proposed late in 1951 that the lesser used piers of Cowal should be closed and services concentrated on the heavy route between Gourock and Dunoon, with Blairmore, the farthest away pier on the Holy Loch station, being served on certain Dunoon sailings.

There was an immediate outcry. The plan was far too radical for its time and the populations of the Cowal villages were not ready to surrender their piers for what was perceived as the economic benefit of a remote Government in London. Dunoon Town Council, and not least Provost Wyatt, were vociferous in their defence of their less

Cargo steamer *Marie* nears Dunoon in May 1948. She was among the last to do so. Dunoon pier received its last call by a cargo boat on 31 October 1949. Road transport was gradually taking hold for freight

A deserted Innellan pier receives an evening call from *Jupiter* as the cruise steamer from Campbeltown passes up firth: ca 1950. Satellite piers such as those on the Holy Loch, at Hunter's Quay, Kirn and Innellan were becoming less frequented because of the advance of road transport

fortunate neighbours. With ill-timing bordering on the crass, a 10% fares increase, though thoroughly justified, was announced just at the height of the piers squabble and this had the effect of uniting all the coast resorts from Campbeltown to Arrochar.

The Minister of Transport, John Maclay, MP for West Renfrew, could not withstand the combined barrage of opposition and caved in, gradually conceding most of the resorts' demands. Although Hunter's Quay was only to be retained as an emergency port when Dunoon was untenable, the other small piers were open for business virtually as usual in the 1952 season. The only advantage to British Rail, and in fact to the travelling public, to accrue from the animosity, was that the paddle steamer (usually the *Caledonia* or *Jupiter*) whch attended mainly to Dunoon, now did so all day and only sailed up from Rothesay in the early morning and back down in the evening. The frequency of sailings to and from Dunoon was increased significantly. At last the vision of the Dunoon Commissioners in the 1880s was being realised and the resort now had a ferry almost wholly dedicated to the Gourock-Dunoon run. This of course was a prerequisite for a point-to-point car ferry service. From October 1952 the departure times from Gourock were standardised at five minutes past the hour and from Dunoon at thirty-five minutes past.

The actual announcement of the coming of the car ferry was made well before the 'Small Piers War'. In February 1951 it was stated that a million pounds was to be spent by BR in modernising their Clyde fleet. Four passenger vessels and three 'dual purpose vessels' were to be built, the latter able to handle cars and cargo at all states of the tide at existing piers. All seven ships were to have diesel rather than steam engines. The days of the traditional Clyde steamer were numbered. Gradually the older turbines and paddle steamers were to be withdrawn from service, starting with the pre-Great War ships.

1952 was an experimental year when regular excursion sailings were cut quite drastically. Two of the cruise steamers, the *Duchess of Montrose* and *Jeanie Deans*, were not placed on regular rosters but largely gave locally advertised trips on an occasional basis. The black-boards outside Dunoon Kiosk or the pages of the *Dunoon Observer* had to be scanned for information on their sailings. The venture was not entirely successful and was modified in subsequent seasons. What the new adjustable timetable did produce was a return to the evening cruises so beloved of the thirties when for a remarkably cheap fare one of the excursion steamers would sail after her normal day's work was done down the firth or up the lochs. Later one of the Glasgow evening newspapers sponsored a series of such cruises known as the "*Evening Citizen* Showboats". The refreshment rooms on board usually did a roaring trade.

Dunoon had two unusual callers this year. At one end of the spectrum a motor vessel had been brought overland from Loch Awe to work the lightly loaded Holy Loch run in winter, and to give her useful employment during the summer season the little *Countess of Breadal-bane* was used in a variety of novel ways. On several days she was based at Dunoon to give special hourly short cruises round the firth. Tickets could only be purchased at the Information Kiosk and for 1/6 (just over 7p) the tripper received a two-portion ticket, one portion for pier dues. The *Countess*, being very cheap on fuel and having a small crew, was able to reinstate the late evening train connection runs to and from Dunoon which had lapsed since the war and for one year only an early morning Sunday run. She thus became very popular with the Town Council, who had been pressing for these concessions for some time. In order to assist embarkation on to the *Countess* at low water a "cattle ramp" was cut away from the face of the south berth the following year.

At the other end of the spectrum Dunoon received a return call from the Isle of Man Steam Packet Company's turbine steamer *Tynwald*, which at 330 feet is thought to be the largest vessel ever to

New acquisition *Countess of Breadalbane* draws near to Dunoon. This motor vessel was used from 1952 to work the lightly used Holy Loch run in winter and for cruises in summer

The largest ship ever to call at Dunoon: TS *Tynwald* from Belfast

Geoffrey Grimshaw collection: Courtesy of the McLean Museum, Greenock

berth at the pier. She brought 2000 excursionists from Belfast. Despite problems in berthing due to a falling tide – and fairly incessant rain – the outing was voted a huge success and hundreds lined the pier promenade to see her go at eight o'clock in the evening. The previous June the *Tynwald* had called for the first time on a similar voyage. On that occasion the main news centered round the patronage received by shops and stalls selling ice cream, teas and 'novelties' – but most of all shortbread.

1953 saw the first batch of the long promised new vessels arrive on the Clyde. Their names were deliberately different from any of the old steamers, signifying a break with the past. The *Maids of Ashton, Argyll, Skelmorlie* and *Cumbrae* were used for inter-resort sailings in the upper firth, for afternoon and evening cruises and as a back up to the larger steamers on the ferry crossings. They even introduced the concept of the "Café Cruise" which was a forenoon trip which included the novelty of a 'free' cup of coffee and a chocolate biscuit. Their

A very new *Maid of Cumbrae* lying at the old goods berth on her Glasgow-Dunoon excursion in July 1953

advantages over the traditional steamers were their undoubted economy in operation, their suitability as comfortable winter craft and their manoeuvrability at piers. On the down side, however, was the inevitable vibration associated with a diesel ship and the fact that there was not a great deal of accommodation if a full complement was being carried. One wag christened them the "Maids of Plywood".

Dunoon received calls from all four vessels and in fact in 1953 the *Maid of Cumbrae* had the Cowal resort as her destination on All the Way trips from Glasgow. With the traditional cruise steamers all back on full rosters and the introduction of the versatile Maids the programme of full day and shorter cruises positively mushroomed.

The more significant event, however, occurred the following year. While the "Maids" could not be described as traditional Clyde steamers they were nevertheless conventional vessels. The car ferries were revolutionary. The first of the batch, the *Arran*, was lying at Gourock ready for service at the end of 1953. Instead of a mainmast she had a pair of samson posts supporting derricks and aft of the passenger accommodation there was an electrical hoist connected to side ramps which allowed vehicles to be embarked and disembarked at all states of the tide. The hoist would lower five cars at a time down to a spacious garage, equipped with turntable, at main deck level.

Over the New Year the paddle steamer *Waverley* was on the Gourock-Dunoon service. A greater contrast could hardly be imagined when at 12.10 pm on 4 January 1954 the *Arran* left Berth A at Gourock Pier with twelve cars aboard for Dunoon. The townsfolk of Dunoon, taking advantage of the suspension of pier dues for the day, were out in force to greet her at half past twelve as she took the north berth at the pier and they allegedly cheered loudly as she approached. Lord Inverclyde, as the representative of the Scottish Tourist Board, cut a white ribbon to allow the first car, driven by the Secretary of the Royal Scottish Automobile Club, to drive ashore.

The car ferry *Arran* on her inaugural run to Dunoon: 4 January 1954

Fares were slashed and a car less than 12hp could now travel over for 15/- (75p); for the first time return tickets were available at one and a half times the single fare. The *Arran's* success was immediate and outstripped all predictions. By the end of January over 400 vehicles had crossed. On 23 March the 2000th driver was presented with a free ticket; on 3 July the 10,000th driver was presented not only with a free ticket but also with a travelling rug and was invited by the Provost to the Council Chambers to sign the visitors' book.

Fortunately by Easter weekend that year the second dual-purpose vessel *Cowal* was ready for service. Dunoon had the busiest Easter in years. From the names of the three 'ABC' ferries, *Arran, Bute* and *Cowal*, it is obvious that BR had assumed that each ferry would serve the station after which she had been named. In the event Dunoon alone needed the services of two ferries most of the time at least during the high season.

The transport of goods was also revolutionised. Cargo was now loaded on to three ton containers at a goods depot in Glasgow and taken by rail to Gourock. There the containers were run on to the ferries on bogeys drawn by so-called 'mechanical horses'. At Dunoon they were taken off by similar means and unloaded in the goods shed ready for distribution. The advantages over the time-honoured method of carriage on open barrows were obvious.

A rather sleek specimen is unloaded at Dunoon: ca 1965. The arrival of the US base in the Holy Loch brought such automobiles to Dunoon

The extract from the programme of cruises from Dunoon during the peak 1955 season

AFTERNOON CRUISES

		CRUISE FARE
MONDAYS, 27th June, 11th and 25th July, 8th and 22nd August By P.S. "Caledonia"	Leaving DUNOON at 12.5 p.m. Arriving back at 4.0 p.m.	
To LOCHGOILHEAD		4/6
MONDAYS, 4th and 18th July, 1st, 15th and 29th August By T.S. "Duchess of Montrose" (P.S. "Caledonia" on 4th July and 29th August)	Leaving DUNOON at 12.5 p.m. Arriving back at 4.0 p.m.	CRUISE FARE
To ARROCHAR		5/-
MONDAYS to FRIDAYS By P.S. "Jeanie Deans"	Leaving DUNOON at 1.25 p.m. and INNELLAN at 1.45 p.m.	CRUISE FARE
ROUND ISLAND OF BUTE		7/-
Arriving back INNELLAN at 5.40 p.m. and DUNOON at 6.0 p.m.		
MONDAYS to SATURDAYS		CRUISE FARE
To KYLES OF BUTE (TIGHNABRUAICH)		5/-

OUTWARD	p.m.	SO 1 20	RETURN	p.m.	SX p.m.	SO p.m.
Dunoon ....leave	1 20	2 55	Tighnabruaich ....leave	3 55	4 15	5 40
Innellan .... "		3 15	Innellan ....arrive		5 40	7 5
Tighnabruaich ....arrive	2 55	4 35	Dunoon .... "	5 25	6 0	7 25
SX—Saturdays excepted			SO—Saturdays only			

		CRUISE FARE
MONDAYS and FRIDAYS		By "Maid of Cumbrae"
To LARGS 4/- and ROTHESAY 4/6		
Leaving HUNTER'S QUAY 2.0 p.m., KIRN 2.5 p.m. and DUNOON 2.15 p.m. Arriving back at DUNOON 5.50 p.m., KIRN 5.55 p.m. and HUNTER'S QUAY 6.0 p.m.		
MONDAYS and FRIDAYS By "Maid of Skelmorlie"		CRUISE FARE
To LOCH LONG and GARE LOCH		4/6
Leaving DUNOON at 2.45 p.m. and KIRN 2.50 p.m. Arriving back KIRN 5.40 p.m., and DUNOON 5.45 p.m.		
TUESDAYS		By "Maid of Cumbrae"
To LARGS 4/-, MILLPORT 4/-, DUNAGOIL BAY 4/6		
Leaving HUNTER'S QUAY 2.0 p.m., KIRN 2.5 p.m. and DUNOON 2.15 p.m. Arriving back at DUNOON 5.50 p.m., KIRN 5.55 p.m. and HUNTER'S QUAY 6.0 p.m.		
TUESDAYS By "Maid of Skelmorlie"		CRUISE FARE
To LOCH LONG	Leaving DUNOON at 3.5 p.m. Arriving back at 44.5 p.m.	2/6
WEDNESDAYS		By "Maid of Cumbrae"
To LARGS 4/-, MILLPORT 4/-, KILCHATTAN BAY 4/6		
Leaving HUNTER'S QUAY 1.45 p.m., KIRN 1.50 p.m. and DUNOON 2.0 p.m. Arriving back at DUNOON 5.50 p.m., KIRN 5.55 p.m. and HUNTER'S QUAY 6.0 p.m.		
WEDNESDAYS By P.S. "Waverley"		CRUISE FARE
To LOCH GOIL (CARRICK CASTLE)		2/6
Leaving DUNOON at 2.45 p.m. and KIRN 2.50 p.m. Arriving back at KIRN 4.35 p.m. and DUNOON 4.45 p.m.		
THURSDAYS		By "Maid of Cumbrae"
To LARGS 4/-, MILLPORT 4/-, CRUISE ROUND CUMBRAE 4/6		
Leaving HUNTER'S QUAY 2.0 p.m., KIRN 2.5 p.m. and DUNOON 2.15 p.m. Arriving back at DUNOON 5.50 p.m., KIRN 5.55 p.m. and HUNTER'S QUAY 6.0 p.m.		
THURSDAYS By "Maid of Skelmorlie"		CRUISE FARE
To GARE LOCH	Leaving DUNOON at 3.5 p.m. Arriving back at 4.45 p.m.	2/6
MONDAYS, TUESDAYS and FRIDAYS (6th June until 5th September) By M.V. "Countess of Breadalbane"		CRUISE FARE
To HOLY LOCH	Leaving DUNOON at 3.15 p.m. Arriving back at 4.40 p.m.	2/-
SATURDAYS		By "Maid of Argyll"
To LOCHGOILHEAD 4/6 and ARROCHAR 5/-		
Leaving DUNOON 12.35 p.m., KIRN 12.45 p.m. and HUNTER'S QUAY 12.50 p.m. Arriving back at HUNTER'S QUAY 6.20 p.m., KIRN 6.25 p.m. and DUNOON 6.30 p.m.		
SATURDAYS, 2nd, 9th, 16th and 23rd July, 6th, 13th and 20th August By T.S. "Duchess of Montrose"		CRUISE FARE
CRUISE ROUND AILSA CRAIG	Leaving DUNOON at 2.20 p.m. Arriving back at 8.20 p.m.	7/6

Rise and fall

1955 proved to be the zenith of the post-war period. The weather was warm and glorious – following a severe thunder storm in early July no further rain fell until late September. On a Wednesday morning in July, for example, between nine and ten, one could be forgiven for imagining that the thirties had returned. Berth A would take the *Maid* from Craigendoran connecting into the cruise steamers and proceeding on to Innellan and Rothesay before it was occupied by the car ferry loading passengers, vehicles and goods for Gourock (the third run of the day). A veritable procession would berth in turn at the south berth: first the *Duchess of Hamilton* bound for Arran via the Kyles of Bute, then the *Duchess of Montrose* for Lochranza and Campbeltown, the *Waverley* for Round the Lochs and Firth of Clyde and finally the red-funnelled *Saint Columba* bound for Tarbert and Ardrishaig with connections for Islay and Oban and the North.

Neil McGilp the announcer had his work cut out for him trying to direct passengers to the outside, middle and inside queues forming alongside the tearoom.

It was around this time that the Caledonian Steam Packet Company, dormant in the public eye since 1923, came back into the limelight – the CSP houseflag was once again flown, seaman's jerseys were emblazoned with the CSP insignia and CSP replaced British Railways in advertisements.

A further high point for Dunoon occurred on 11 August 1958 when HM the Queen and the Duke of Edinburgh visited the Burgh. A set of steps at the rear of the tearoom at the south berth had been specially built for the occasion and were appropriately christened the Queen's Steps. Her Majesty sailed from *Britannia* to the pier and was officially welcomed by the Secretary of State for Scotland, the Lord Lieutenant of Argyll, the Sheriff Principal for Argyll and Provost Wyatt. She went on, incidentally, to unveil a commemorative plaque at the newly constructed Pavilion across the Esplanade, a structure replacing one lost by fire almost ten years previously and subsequently renamed the Queen's Hall.

Although the Queen did not return to Dunoon she was in the Clyde in August 1965 to review the Home Fleet lying at anchor at the Tail of

As foreign package holidays came to have a greater appeal, the excursion traffic declined from the mid-50s – here a packed *Saint Columba* berths at Dunoon on her last day in service: 27 September 1958

the Bank. Dunoon Pier was a seething mass of humanity in the early evening as every few minutes a steamer left to take trippers round the naval ships, listing dangerously as they approached. All the remaining paddle steamers, together with the *Duchess of Hamilton*, the *Maid of Ashton* and even the car ferry *Arran* were pressed into service to cope with the crowds.

If there is a high point there follows an inevitable deterioration. In the case of the weather, with the exception of 1959, this was the case, but excursion traffic also fell away, thanks to the attraction of the ever more sought-after package holidays abroad. As the older steamers became more and more expensive to maintain and were seen to approach the end of their useful lives they were sadly withdrawn from service. During the late fifties and early sixties – incorporating the Beeching years – many of the old favourites found their way to the breaker's yard, not least the *Saint Columba, Duchess of Montrose* and *Jeanie Deans*. The old 'ferry class' steamers had been already declared redundant by the coming of the *Maids* and car ferries.

The small piers too needed a great deal of remedial work and with traffic falling quite substantially they too closed one by one. In fact by the early seventies Dunoon was the only pier left in regular use in the whole Cowal peninsula. Dunoon Pier's closest neighbour, Kirn, closed in December 1963; the car ferry *Cowal* was the last ship to call and on that day landed a vehicle at the pier for the first time for many a long day – a hearse.

During this period there occurred an event which, until 1 November 1960 when it was announced in Parliament, had been totally unpredicted – the arrival in the Holy Loch of the United States nuclear submarine depot ship *Proteus*. With over a thousand American seamen, many with families, having to find accommodation in Cowal, the makeup of Dunoon's population did change. Perhaps in one way, this was a blessing as one of the main concerns of all the Clyde resorts at

An idyllic summer afternoon as spectators on the promenade watch the *Caledonia* cast off (the fog bell is clearly seen): early 1960s

this time was the downturn in the tourist industry. The Provosts had sought and eventually obtained a meeting with the Secretary of State for Scotland in which they pleaded with him to influence British Railways to change their fare structure in order to increase carryings. He later replied in writing that it was outwith his power to do so and in fact a further fares increase was imposed and further retrenchment planned. As in the forties, fares had quite simply not kept up with inflation.

Thanks to the fact that Dunoon pier was now also a car ferry terminal, vehicular traffic at least remained steady or even continued its upward trend. In the early sixties, following complaints from the regular travellers, action had to be taken to prevent important railway connection services like the 1810 ex Gourock being delayed by vehicle traffic. As the car ferry could not turn round any faster the way out was to have the service duplicated by a *Maid* carrying passengers only. Similarly the 1135 ex Dunoon, a run where many travellers had rail connections furth of Glasgow, was duplicated by a passenger only vessel. By 1968 nearly 80,000 vehicles were crossing between Gourock and Dunoon.

New owners and new ferries

The Clyde steamers and ferries ceased to be under railway control on Hogmanay 1968. From New Year's Day the Caledonian Steam Packet Company became a wholly owned subsidiary of the bus-dominated Scottish Transport Group. By July 1969 the Scottish Transport Group also had control of David MacBrayne Ltd. The ultimate authority was now the Secretary of State for Scotland rather than the Minister of Transport in London.

Far-reaching developments occurred thick and fast as the new management tried to get to grips with the realities of transport in the late twentieth century. Although the two companies continued to be administered separately their vessels were treated as if they belonged to one fleet. Within two years there was an almost complete withdrawal of the old ships: the red funnel was seen for the last time on the mail run to and from Tarbert and Ardrishaig, well over a century since the day the Edinburgh postmaster first timed the performance of the *Dolphin* as she left the mails behind at Dunoon. The favourite steamer *Caledonia* and even the immensely popular *Duchess of Hamilton* did not survive.

Dunoon now only had two excursion steamers – the turbine *Queen Mary II* on day cruises and the paddle steamer *Waverley* sailing largely in the afternoon.

A comprehensive review of their shipping empire in the winter of 1969/70 made the new STG Board realise that the great priority for West Coast services was the provision of 'roll-on roll-off' facilities where the need for a hoist was obviated and inordinate delays, especially at low water, eliminated. The problem of course was capital expenditure as new vessels and new terminals incorporating linkspans were needed. Dunoon Town Council was consulted and plans prepared for a projected terminal at the pier.

The cost was prohibitive and, despite their enthusiasm for the project, the Councillors naturally hesitated before spending so much public money. Fortunately a 50% Government grant was available thanks to the Congested Districts (Scotland) Act of 1897. The initial plans submitted to the Scottish Office were, however, rejected as being too grandiose and a more basic design was to be produced. In the design

MacBrayne interloper: the Skye ferry
Clansman on the Dunoon run: 1970 – the
largest and finest ship ever to appear on the
Gourock-Dunoon run was popular with
commuters and trippers alike

of Messrs Crouch & Hogg, the civil engineers, the harbour jetty was to
be extended in an arc to the north end of the pier, ending in a dolphin
and loading ramp. A cheaper alternative had to be found.

Meanwhile the ships on the Gourock-Dunoon run were changing.
In November 1969 the pioneer car ferry *Arran* was withdrawn from
Clyde service and transferred on charter to MacBrayne's hoist-loading
service to Islay. MacBrayne's had built a new drive-through ferry for
this particular service but as she was unable to use the existing
terminals it was agreed that she would be chartered to the CSP as a
quid pro quo for use as the Dunoon ferry. To maintain the service for
the first five months of 1970 until this new *Iona* was ready the CSP
chartered the spare MacBrayne ferry *Clansman*. Still manned by a
MacBrayne crew (except for the purser) but with her red funnel
repainted yellow, the largest and finest ship ever to appear on the
Gourock-Dunoon run was popular with commuters and trippers alike.
With her greater size of hoist and garage she was able to increase the
commercial traffic carried between the two terminals, although often

The Caledonian Steam Packet Co Ltd

The 1970 hovercraft initiative can be seen as HM2-011 impressively speeds across the firth as the *Iona* lies at the south berth at Dunoon. Like previous attempts to develop hover services this one foundered because of problems with the weather and mechanical trouble

at the expense of her timekeeping. The *Iona* herself went into service at the end of May. With bow visor, hoist and stern ramp she was the first drive-through vessel in Clyde service. These facilities could not of course all be used but her capacity for 47 cars could certainly be turned to good account. Sensibly her turnround times were increased to three quarters of an hour, but even this leisurely schedule could not at all times be met. A *Maid* was brought in to ensure that train connections were met and the car ferry *Bute* gave additional crossings morning and evening. Dunoon had never had it so good.

An even more unconventional vessel made its appearance at Dunoon in 1970. The Scottish Transport Group had announced that they wished to see hovercraft services develop on the Clyde. Just as the *Iona* was taking up service a Southampton-built craft was showing its paces off Gourock. With a cruising speed of 35 knots and a passenger capacity for 65 the future looked good for *HM2-011*, especially as the fares to be charged were not too steep. From 4 July she included Dunoon in her daily schedule, loading at the Queen's Steps behind the pier. Dunoon Town Council had been consulted about her berthing at the pier but had delayed giving permission as the Councillors were afraid that they might incur expenditure on an experimental service already in receipt of a government grant. Because of bad weather and mechanical unreliability the service turned out to be hardly a success and quietly lapsed after the 1971 season. It could be said that this was Dunoon's one and only air service – the vessel was classified as an aircraft and her passenger certificate issued by the Air Registration Board.

This was in fact the second attempt to introduce hovercraft services to the Clyde. Back in 1965 a firm called Clyde Hover Ferries Ltd introduced two SRN6 types to the unsuspecting public. Trials at 55 knots were deemed successful and in August of that year an eight minute crossing time was offered between Gourock and Dunoon. Landing was not at the pier but on the beach adjoining. Unfortunately the craft was excessively noisy. Allegedly irate residents complained that ornaments were being shaken from house walls, golfers were being put off their putts and churchgoers could not hear the minister's sermon. Complaints even reached Westminster. It was, however, poor traffic figures and unreliable weather which finally put an end to a courageous experiment.

Roll-on roll-off

The sale in 1969 of the closed pier at Hunter's Quay to a charity known as Dunoon Nominees Ltd as a speculative venture did not attract a great deal of publicity. At that time a private company, Western Ferries Ltd, was making inroads into MacBrayne's Islay traffic using simple, unsophisticated ships and terminals combined with minimal crewing. Western Ferries soon announced that they themselves were involved in the Hunter's Quay deal and that they proposed to run a service from there to a point near the Cloch Lighthouse employing a style of operation similar to their Islay venture. Early in 1970 they obtained permission to build terminals at Hunter's Quay and at McInroy's Point on the Renfrewshire coast, but no building work commenced right away.

At the same time Dunoon Town Council were in debate with the Scottish Transport Group and the Scottish Office over the future of Dunoon Pier, the first submission for a linkspan having been turned down. Western Ferries had already intimated to the Council that they considered their own terminal more economical than modifying the Burgh Pier. They soon announced that they were intending to open their competitive route in the following spring. In a change of heart, or more likely with a degree of prompting, Mr Rose, Manager of Western Ferries, intimated to the Council in November 1971 that his Company would after all be prepared to erect a utility terminal at the north end of Dunoon Pier providing it would cost no more than at Hunter's Quay.

The plans of the new ramp at Dunoon as they were published in the press: 1971

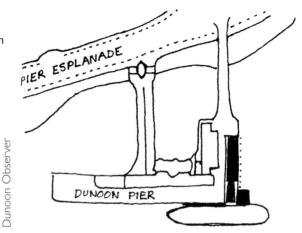

Dunoon Observer

What might have been –
Western Ferries offered to
sail into Dunoon pier but on
the casting vote of the
Provost, Dunoon Town
Council opted for the
Scottish Transport Group
scheme to build a side-
loading ramp. Here, the
Highland Seabird is seen at
the pier with the *Queen
Mary* in 1976

Gregor Roy collection

The Scottish Transport Group warned the Council that acceptance of the Western Ferries' scheme would prejudice the future of the CSP service from Gourock. The Town Council was split down the middle but eventually, in early December, they agreed to the STG-approved scheme – but only on the casting vote of the Provost. An adjustable side-loading ramp would be grafted on to the north end of the existing pier at a cost of £150,000. The half not paid by the Government would be advanced by the STG, who in return would not be charged berthing dues at Dunoon for fourteen years.

There was opposition, some questioning the use of public money when Western Ferries had been willing to pay and others doubting the wisdom of a scheme which ultimately would have to be converted to the full drive-through system.

An end-loading ramp had already been installed at Gourock Pier. Completed in July 1971, it had been hanselled by the *Iona*. Vehicles were loaded by the stern but because of the difficulties of disembarking at Dunoon large commercials still had to be side-loaded by hoist. The *Iona's* charter to the CSP was only temporary and she was urgently needed for service in the Western Isles. On 3 November, therefore, she bade a temporary farewell to Dunoon. Her place was taken by the *Glen Sannox*, originally employed on the Arran service and subsequently modified to end-loading with the addition of a stern ramp. A special bollard was constructed to take her bow rope at Dunoon.

From early in 1972 passengers and cars suffered the inconvenience of pier works. At last Messrs Baird Brothers of Port Glasgow, having been awarded the contract, had been able to start on the installation of the vehicular ramp and causeway at the goods entrance to the pier. A concrete dolphin also had to be provided to the north of the linkspan for the ferry's stern and waist ropes and to assist berthing while a spring fender would have to be put in place along the front to safeguard the pier when the ferry came alongside.

In fact when the new structure was opened, on 31 March, just in time for Easter, the *Iona* was back on the run, the *Sannox* having gone for further modifications. It was the *Glen Sannox*, however, which transported none other than Miss Scotland across the firth to do the honours at the official opening on 12 July. No doubt the officials waiting on the pier could keep in touch with the approaching ferry – a VHF radio telephone system had been installed throughout the firth and the fleet for ship to pier contact.

The ferry now ran to time, but traffic had reached such proportions that one ship alone was insufficient. The original plan had been that the *Arran*, supposedly redundant from the Islay station, would act as a 'pup' and between her and the *Glen Sannox* provide a 45 minute service. When a public enquiry put paid to that idea and the Arran was no longer available, the ingenious idea was seized upon to modify the little *Maid of Cumbrae*, also lying spare, to take her place. Her superstructure was cut away to main deck level aft of the funnel and a stern ramp and two side ramps fitted so that fifteen small cars could be accommodated on the open deck and the alleyways round the engine room.

That summer, 1972, seventeen double runs were offered between the two terminals. A revised fare system was put into effect to encourage traffic, special reduced day returns were introduced and advance booking of vehicles was no longer necessary. In winter too a 45 minute service was still in place although this was later modified when the *Maid* had to cover in addition the transport of Admiralty workers to and from Kilcreggan.

Edward Quinn

The first call at Dunoon of the *Glen Sannox*, before she was altered for the regular
service: 8 March 1970

Cars embarking on to the
Maid of Cumbrae using
Dunoon's new linkspan:
1972

New ferries and a bit of opposition

The promised Western Ferries link between Hunter's Quay and McInroy's Point materialised in 1973. On 3 June a former Swedish ro-ro ferry, rejuvenated and renamed *Sound of Shuna*, was placed on the station and offered an hourly drive-through service. Joined a month or so later by a similar red-hulled ferry, the *Sound of Scarba*, a half-hour frequency became possible at weekends.

Despite a severe setback when in September the McInroy's Point linkspan was destroyed in a gale the service took hold and the traditional crossing to Dunoon Pier began to lose some traffic.

Piermaster J H Beatty had never had to contend with this opposition problem. He entered into well-deserved retirement on 21 May, to be replaced later by Kenneth McArthur. Captain McArthur, however, held the position for only two years: he 'returned to the sea' by becoming a master with Western Ferries and his place was taken by Robert Reid.

From 1 January 1973 the CSP combined with MacBrayne's and was renamed Caledonian MacBrayne Ltd, the Clyde and Western Isles Divisions being created to deal with the concerns of the two former separate entities. The new company had already announced that the *Maid of Cumbrae* would offer late runs at the height of the season and that twenty-journey car tickets, valid for one month, would also be available. Less than a week after the introduction of the Western Ferries service, new lower car rates were announced on the Dunoon service, the size variation in charging was removed and the limited validity of the ten-journey ticket was discontinued. Ten-journey tickets were in fact extended to passengers some six months later. Obviously, Caledonian MacBrayne were taking the opposition very seriously indeed.

Just after the go ahead for the Dunoon linkspan had been given by the Town Council at the end of 1971 the contract for a purpose-built vessel for the new service had been awarded to Lamont's of Port Glasgow. With capacity for up to 36 cars and four hundred passengers the new ship was to be given bow thrusters and Voith Schneider propulsion units fore and aft. These would provide her with greater manoeuvrability and would propel her at the rate of some 14 knots. She was launched as *Jupiter* by the wife of Cal Mac's General Manager

A newly reconditioned *Sound of Scarba* at Western Ferries' linkspan at Hunter's Quay: 1973

The first of the 'streakers', MV *Jupiter* on her speed trials: 12 March 1974

James Hall, Greenock

The twins at Dunoon, *Jupiter* (left) and *Juno*: January 1975

in November 1973 and finally entered service on a very wet morning on 19 March. On trial she had reached 15.5 knots ahead, 13 knots astern and an amazing 3 knots sideways. With her ability 'to pirouette' on berthing she could achieve very fast turnrounds and could cope with an hourly interval service on what was described as the 'Marine Motorway' between Gourock and Dunoon.

With assistance from the *Maid of Cumbrae* the service became half-hourly. Late evening sailings were extended and the numbers of high commercial vehicles travelling increased impressively. Contrary to previous predictions the *Jupiter* was granted a passenger certificate for 690 although passengers would be likely to be rather uncomfortable at full complement. By the end of the year car traffic had increased by a remarkable 21,000 and passengers by 58,000.

In a desperate effort to stimulate the economy the Government had permitted the Scottish Transport Group to order a sister ship for the Upper Clyde services. After the launch of the *Juno* on 16 September 1974 by the wife of STG's Managing Director, Chairman Sir Patrick Thomas gave statistics for the Dunoon route: an annual total of a million passengers, 120,000 cars and more than 10,000 coaches. The new ship entered service in early December rendering the *Maid of Cumbrae* redundant, the smaller vessel being used only as the winter 'pup' and during relief periods.

With a new vessel purpose-built for Islay the *Arran*, now end-loading, was also spare. On the occasions she came to Dunoon planks had to be used to assist vehicle embarkation until ramp supports were put in place. With the two new and novel sisters (affectionately known as the 'streakers') normally on duty a very high class service could be given. With fares kept down by competition, the Dunoon folk could not believe their good fortune.

Western Ferries, incidentally, acquired the historic Isle of Wight car ferry *Lymington* and, as *Sound of Sanda*, used her as a spare and relief vessel.

Clyde cruising in the seventies

In the early seventies the cruise steamers sailing out of Dunoon were the *Queen Mary II* and the *Waverley*. By 1973 the financial results were so disappointing, especially in the realms of the full day excursions, that the STG decided that the *Waverley* had to be axed. Her boilers were in a precarious state and needed a great deal of expenditure. Her former base, Craigendoran, had been closed the previous year, ending a particularly long association with Dunoon, it having been the original destination of the Craigendoran steamers nearly a hundred years before.

In 1974, then, the *Mary* was the only excursion steamer left on the Clyde. Dunoon was offered cruises Round the Lochs and Round Bute with a weekly day excursion to Arran. A group of enthusiasts, the Paddle Steamer Preservation Society, had been working very closely with the CSP and Cal Mac to publicise their unique paddle steamer and, in a wonderfully magnanimous gesture, the STG 'donated' the now redundant *Waverley* to the Society for £1. Much to their surprise the Society, thanks to numerous grants and general goodwill, formed a company to operate the paddler, dry-docked and refitted her, painted her funnels in her original LNER red, white and black and, some eighteen months after she had last sailed publicly, took her on her 'maiden voyage' on the firth.

Dunoon featured quite prominently in her cruise timetable. Her season had mixed fortunes, largely thanks to her aged boiler. Retubing of the boiler during her overhaul did the trick and 1976 was a more successful summer. 'Paw, maw and the weans' took her to their collective hearts.

That year Cal Mac were the sole recipients of the new Strathclyde Regional Council's cruising grant and the Company were able to set about an intensive publicity campaign, culminating in their ship's returning to her orginal name *Queen Mary* and, shown the way by the opposition, once again offering All the Way cruises from the centre of Glasgow. Rivalry was quite intense between the two ships and both had their partisan following. For a brief period a new generation learned of the joys and frustrations of competition known to their grandparents.

1976 actually saw a third craft on the Clyde which for part of her roster was very much a cruise vessel. A Western Ferries crew had gone to Norway to bring to the Clyde the catamaran they named *Highland Seabird*. From mid-June she was based at Rothesay and gave commuter runs to Dunoon, Helensburgh and Greenock and even for a short time up river. When not engaged in this work she cruised up the lochs or, on Sundays, round Bute to Tarbert. Despite the lack of open deck space, she was voted quite successful, cruising along at over 25 knots was not unpleasant. She did not reappear the following year.

It was on Glasgow Fair Friday 1977 that the *Waverley* was being turned inside the Gantocks before berthing at Dunoon in an effort to save precious minutes before a prestigious evening charter. Her master rang for full astern to avert running over the red can buoy just north of the rocks, but thanks to the combination of an ebb tide, a slow response to the helm and a list to port as 600 passengers queued up ready to disembark, she stranded while actually going astern, like the *Eclipse* and the 1889 *Caledonia* before her. Passengers were asked to move forward so that an attempt could be made to get off the small pinnacle of rock which she had struck, but to no avail. The *Juno* quickly arrived and hove-to for over an hour until all the passengers had been safely landed at Dunoon Pier, largely by Western Ferries' *Sound of Shuna* which managed alongside. Two tugs tried to pull her off but in fact only succeeded in making matters worse as they slewed the bow round to the north. Water began to pour in aft but a US Navy craft arrived in the nick of time and stemmed the flow of water with her pumps. Fortunately the paddler lifted off on her own at high tide and was able to run, first of all to the Coal Pier adjacent to the steamer pier, and then, the holes sealed with quick-drying cement, to Govan Dry Dock for extensive repairs.

Ironically, the *Waverley* survived after 1977 despite the *contretemps* with the Gantocks. The *Queen Mary* did not. The following year the car ferry *Glen Sannox*, duly re-engined and refurbished, was available to act as cruise 'steamer' for Cal Mac. Giving her a dual function made economic sense – she was still able to act as a car ferry at peak periods and in winter – but despite the Company's best efforts she was never really a success in her new guise. Quite simply, the *Glen Sannox* did not have the charisma of the World's Last Sea-going Paddle Steamer. In 1981 she was limited to 'Inter-Resort' cruising with ferry runs to and from Dunoon morning and evening. This in effect meant she replaced a 'streaker' at busy times and the *Jupiter* was laid up for the summer. From 1982 she herself was mothballed as spare boat and Cal Mac's venture into cruising appeared to be at an end.

Unexpectedly 1985 brought a revival. The passenger motor vessel *Keppel* was no longer required on the route she had worked for almost twenty years, from Largs to Millport. Cal Mac decided to use her to revive cruising in a rather low key fashion. Her limited capacity and her excruciatingly slow speed were disadvantages but she was comfortable and, with an imaginative schedule, was able to offer a satisfactory service. Pensioners, for example, found her very attractive as she wended her leisurely way from Dunoon to Rothesay and the Kyles, Largs and Millport or Carrick Castle in Loch Goil. She lasted in this rôle until 1992 but the following year appeared under the name *Clyde Rose* for a private operator giving broadly similar excurions. This gamble was an abysmal failure – the *Keppel* deserved a better fate.

A few years previously a similar speculative venture had also ended in disaster. The privately owned veteran *Queen of Scots* had offered a variety of cruises and had even berthed overnight at Dunoon, the only vessel ever to have done so on a regular basis.

1985 also saw a welcome though small scale revival of Cal Mac cruising when the *Jupiter* was rostered to sail twice a week from Dunoon, etc to Loch Long or Tighnabruaich. These trips were not renewed in 1986, but in 1993, after the withdrawal of the *Keppel*, a member of the Jupiter class started up midweek cruises to Tighnabruaich offering very cheap fares – £5 with half price for pensioners. The ship would be dressed overall and deck chairs provided. Next year the cruise programme was expanded: a 'streaker' fed into the *Pioneer* at Rothesay from Dunoon and Gourock and a day cruise to Arran became possible after a lapse of several years. In addition Tarbert was the destination on Sundays. With minor modifications this programme continued through the nineties.

The only cruise vessel calling at Dunoon apart from the *Waverley* was now the *Second Snark*, a delightful pre-war product from Denny's yard in Dumbarton. This attractive motor vessel gave inter-resort cruises from Mondays to Fridays during a fairly long summer season, featuring Dunoon almost daily in her varied timetable.

'Cruise steamer' *Keppel* at Dunoon with the *Saturn* at the ferry berth: August 1992

Uncomfortable decisions

As the seventies drew to a close the remaining two of the original Clyde motor vessels of the fifties were finally sold – the *Maid of Cumbrae* and *Arran*. Winter reliefs on the Dunoon service required when the 'streakers' were being overhauled were from the 1979/80 winter in the hands of yet another redundant Islay ferry, the *Pioneer*. Equipped with new side ramps (incorporated into a hoist for her summer employment as Skye ferry) the West Highland vessel did not have the ability to berth as quickly as the *Jupiter* or *Juno* but she was considerably faster between piers and was thus able to keep fairly well to schedule.

A feature of the fare structure in the late seventies had been a summer surcharge on all fares going to Dunoon though not for the locals whose journeys started in Cowal. Both Cal Mac and Western Ferries were parties to this arrangement. Then in 1979 Western Ferries removed their surcharge at the end of August and in fact reduced their fares even further to £2 per car and 75p per passenger. This made their fares cheaper than Cal Mac's and resulted in their capturing a larger share of the traffic – so much so that in winter their half-hour service had to be extended to off-peak periods.

Whether the cause was this upsurge in the traffic carried by Western Ferries or political sympathy for the private sector from a Conservative Secretary of State is unknown but on 2 July 1981 George Younger made an announcement in the House of Commons which caused widespread dismay in certain quarters, not least those who used the route via Dunoon Pier. He stated that he proposed to withdraw the subsidy from Cal Mac for their car and passenger service between Gourock and Dunoon and instead offer a capital grant of £300,000 to Western Ferries to purchase an additional vessel for their McInroy's Point-Hunter's Quay service. Western Ferries were also asked to provide a fast passenger service using their *Highland Seabird* between Gourock and Dunoon. This would attract a subsidy in its first year but if Western Ferries felt unable to continue after this period foot passengers (including those arriving by train) would be taken on a through bus service by the alternative route.

The Scottish Transport Group replied a fortnight later and stated simply that in view of the circumstances they had no alternative but to withdraw the Gourock-Dunoon service after 17 October. The people of Cowal were appalled and dismayed. They gathered forces and by mid-August had sent 376 objections to the Scottish Transport Users' Consultative Committee, the body which dealt with such complaints. A Ferry Services Retention Committee had been formed and spearheaded a demonstration on the pier with lament-playing pipers and the carrying aloft of a black coffin. A packed public enquiry was held in Dunoon on 3 September. The catamaran was condemned both in terms of passenger capacity and suitability in severe weather and Western Ferries were not considered to have sufficient backup for a reliable service.

The 15 page report appeared a fortnight later and stated categorically that if Cal Mac withdrew there would be "serious hardship, inconvenience and difficulty" to the travelling public. Mr Younger had to retract and this he did – partially – in a Commons statement in October. Western Ferries would operate a vehicle service and Cal Mac would carry passengers only.

His minister, Malcolm Rifkind, later 'clarified' the situation by ordering Cal Mac to buy a suitable passenger vessel and if necessary to sell one of the 'streakers'. This was of course no easy task and later he modified his stance by saying that the Government would subsidise a Cal Mac passenger service to Dunoon as long as they competed "in the market place" with Western Ferries for car traffic.

On the basis of the Government's promise Western Ferries proceeded to purchase the diesel electric paddleship *Farringford*, but it was their turn to be non-plussed when Mr Younger announced in February 1982 that he was giving instead £250,000 to Cal Mac to subsidise their passenger service. They had no option but to dispose of their new acquisition. They did, however, purchase another former member of the ex-Lymington-Yarmouth ferries in 1986. She entered service as the *Sound of Seil*.

In fact the Company continued to expand and buy up second-hand tonnage, now from Holland, each acquisition being faster and more commodious than its predecessor. The *Sound of Sleat* joined the fleet in 1988, the *Sound of Scalpay* in 1995 and a new *Sound of Sanda* in 1996. On one occasion there were actually five vessels in service.

Meanwhile the *Jupiter* and *Juno* sailed on until the next crisis. This duly occurred in February 1983 when the Monopolies and Mergers Commission presented their report into Cal Mac to Parliament. They made a considerable number of recommendations but the most important concerning Dunoon was that either the *Jupiter* or the *Juno* was to be disposed of before the summer as only one 'streaker' was required at Dunoon; the revenue gained by the second ship by operating the Ministry of Defence charter for workers to and from Kilcreggan was insufficient to break even. The reaction from the coast was to oppose many of the recommendations. It was felt that this was an accountants' report and took no account of human or social factors. Both ships did in fact continue sailing although many of the Report's other recommendations were carried through. In July 1984 the Secretary of State announced to the Commons that he agreed that the *Jupiter* be retained after all.

The consequence of this whole affair was that Cal Mac were able to compete with the ever-expanding Western Ferries only "with one hand tied behind their back". A second vessel could be used on the Gourock-Dunoon station only as a back up when traffic demanded it or at specific peak times. The fares of the two companies had to be virtually identical, although both had agents in Dunoon and its suburbs selling ten journey tickets at substantial discounts.

By now the rosters of the 'streakers' were fairly standard. One tended to be thirled to Dunoon all day while the other vessel on the so-called No 1A Roster gave the charter service runs to Kilcreggan, Dunoon runs morning and evening and Rothesay or other reliefs as required. From 1986 the third 'streaker' *Saturn*, some three years younger than the other two and hitherto confined to the Rothesay-Wemyss Bay service, took her place at Dunoon as the three exchanged rosters monthly.

The three products of the seventies were beginning to show their age and in 1992/93 received a major refurbishment internally. The passenger lounges were recast tastefully with seats round coffee tables and the whole area became No Smoking. A couple of years later the catering service was withdrawn, apparently because it was losing money, and vending machines installed as replacements. Unfortunately while they worked perfectly on land they tended to break down if not kept horizontal! Having sensed the degree of opposition Cal Mac decided to franchise the catering out to a private firm: the travelling public hardly noticed the difference although the quality of doughnuts was not quite the same.

Incidentally in April 1990 Caledonian MacBrayne had yet another change of ownership. The firm was transferred under the direct control of the Secretary of State for Scotland. The Scottish Bus Group, the main subsidiary of the Scottish Transport Group, had been privatised. The Conservative Government made strenuous efforts to privatise Cal Mac also but following a consultants' report they felt unable to proceed down this line. The coast resorts breathed a collective sigh of relief.

Developments at the pier

As the years rolled by Dunoon Pier began to show its age. For about four decades little changed except perhaps for the colour of paint. The additions of 1937 stood the test of time. To the right, or south, of the passenger gangway was the tearoom; to the left was the waiting room, the toilets and, at an angle, the goods shed leading on to the original gangway or goods entrance. At the level of the promenade cum verandah and just behind it was the piermaster's office while in the south corner stood the signal tower with its loudspeaker playing music and relaying announcements. At the esplanade end of the gangway was the rather handsome building holding the turnstiles for pier dues, at tuppence one way, and just to the north of this stood the diminutive information kiosk. In 1958 the Queen's Steps had been built on at the rear of the tearoom.

By the late fifties a fair amount of remedial work was seen to be necessary and a fair amount of recrimination took place when it was realised that the money spent on the pier per annum since the war was less than pre-war and no fund had been built up for repairs. Between the wars Pier Convener Turner had accumulated a contingency fund but this had been dissipated in dredging on the off-chance that an Irish boat might come to the pier. (This had of course happened only twice). The catalyst for the extensive work was a storm in November 1959 when the vehicle gangway was pounded by the sea and the gatekeeper's hut damaged. A fundamental review of the state of the pier was ordered by the Council. At the very end of 1960 the decision was taken to go ahead with a major reconstruction over two winters, so as to cause minimum interference with the summer traffic.

The work was started by HM Murray & Co Ltd in September 1961 and the first phase completed the following April. This comprised extensive repiling and resurfacing of the goods gangway and the strengthening of the existing structure at the north end of the pier, rather more work being required than had been anticipated. New pier offices and a new goods shed, where vehicles could load under cover, were erected to the right of the gangway. This had the additional benefit of giving more space for the marshalling of cars.

It was October 1962 before the second phase commenced. Right

More room for manoeuvre
following alterations to the pier
in the early 1960s

through until the following Easter large-scale repairs took place at the south of the pier, all the lower timbers being replaced, even those defective ones under the tearoom. Approval was given to convert the former pier offices into a shop and the lessee of the tearoom was given permission to sell it as a going concern. By the end of the summer all the pier buildings had been tastefully repainted. All the efforts and expenditure (nearly £64,000) seemed to have been worth it when a letter appeared in Rothesay's local paper the *Buteman* extolling the virtues of Dunoon Pier compared with Rothesay.

The next change occurred on 1 July 1965 when pier dues were incorporated into the steamer ticket. The Council took advantage of this by raising the pontage from 4d, to which it had gradually climbed, to 6d, although this was offset by the CSP's commission of 10% for collecting the money. The following year it was decided that a ticket vending machine for promenaders should be sited at the pier entrance, the turnstiles were removed and the office became for a while the Tourist Information Centre. Unfortunately the new gates proved to be inadequate as several youths were gaining "unauthorised entry" to the pier. The gap between the gates and the roof had to be filled in.

At the same time the stairs to the balcony under the signal box were cured of dampness and a new left luggage office opened. In June 1968 a fire occurred in the tearoom when some rubbish caught alight in cartons awaiting collection, while in July three years later the woodwork on the landward side of the promenade deck was ablaze. Fortunately the pier staff acted very promptly on each occasion.

The last time the pier signals were actually in use was in 1970/71 while announcements from the signal tower ceased in 1972, the gramophone record turntable being transferred to the piermaster's office. The linkspan, dolphin and other necessary adjuncts to roll-on roll-off were completed in 1972. The pier, owned by the Burgh of Dunoon since 1896, became the property of Strathclyde Regional

The balcony removed – the *Jupiter* berthed and the *Waverley* leaving in 1989

Council following the change of local government in 1975. The new Council continued to be diligent in their attention to matters concerning their new acquisition. Meanwhile the woodwork of the promenade was deteriorating and eventually, in the late seventies, the area had to be condemned for safety reasons. About the same time the tearoom closed on the expiry of the lease to the McKechnies who had run it successfully for years.

Strathclyde Regional Council announced in May 1980 that £175,000 should be spent on upgrading the facilities at Dunoon Pier. They hoped that the Historic Buildings Council would pay 50% and Argyll & Bute District Council agreed to contribute £10,000. In the event Historic Buildings gave less than expected and the work had to be scaled down. Nevertheless by 1982 the building on the south berth which had held the tearoom had been converted into a waiting room with toilets, clean and bright if a little sparsely furnished.

At the south of the main pier building there already existed a bar from which emanated fairly loud disco music. At the time of the renovations police objected to the licence of Mr Harjinder Singh Sangha being renewed on the basis that a certain rowdiness appeared to be prevalent in the vicinity of his premises but they lost their case. The bar survived for a further five years or so.

The piermaster's office had been transferred to a Portakabin behind the goods shed but was very well placed for checking goods and vehicles coming off the ramp. The main change, however, was the demolition of the promenade balcony which commenced in March 1982. Not long after work had started officials realised that the timbers were in a much better state than had been imagined but a last ditch effort to have second thoughts and reinstate the balcony failed on grounds of cost. The two pier buildings became separated. In fact the overall effect was not unlike the original in 1897. The empty signal tower became the property of HM Coastguard.

Major storm damage in the 1990s required expensive repairs. The south building was closed off and the protective screen on the passenger gangway was removed. Winter seas can cause breaks in service because of docking difficulties. Public opinion supports an upgrading of Dunoon pier and Dunoon traders and shopkeepers would not like to see the traffic missing the centre of the town entirely as would happen if Hunter's Quay alone remained

Robert E Reid

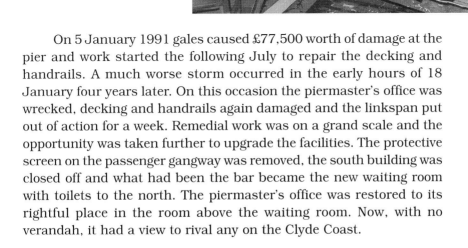

On 5 January 1991 gales caused £77,500 worth of damage at the pier and work started the following July to repair the decking and handrails. A much worse storm occurred in the early hours of 18 January four years later. On this occasion the piermaster's office was wrecked, decking and handrails again damaged and the linkspan put out of action for a week. Remedial work was on a grand scale and the opportunity was taken further to upgrade the facilities. The protective screen on the passenger gangway was removed, the south building was closed off and what had been the bar became the new waiting room with toilets to the north. The piermaster's office was restored to its rightful place in the room above the waiting room. Now, with no verandah, it had a view to rival any on the Clyde Coast.

And finally . . .

During the centenary year of the opening of the double berthed pier at Dunoon, owned since April 1996 by Argyll and Bute Council, serious negotiations were going on about the future of the service between Renfrewshire and Cowal, the whole matter being studied by consultants. The vessels operating the Gourock-Dunoon run for Cal Mac were over twenty years old while the Western Ferries' ships were ten years older even than that, although, having been re-engined, they were classified as new vessels.

The Upper Clyde estuary, Dunoon and Rothesay, had been starved of new investment but until the problem of two companies competing for the same traffic was ironed out no Government could be expected to advance money willingly. The distribution of traffic had been static for some time – 70% to Western Ferries and 30% to Cal Mac. Both companies had built up a loyal following and these percentages would be unlikely to change appreciably. The experience of the early eighties suggested that a passenger only ferry to Dunoon with the vehicles going to Hunter's Quay was unacceptable. While the cost of reconditioning and converting Dunoon Pier, a Grade A-listed building, to end-loading tenable in all weathers would be high, the Dunoon traders and shopkeepers would not like to see the traffic missing the centre of the town entirely as would happen if Hunter's Quay alone remained.

Talk of a possible breakwater to shield the pier from south westerly gales had been in the air for some time. In the end a political decision would have to be made.

One factor in the equation which cannot be ignored is what happens when Dunoon comes alive on the last Saturday in August each summer. Thousands flock to the ferries to reach Dunoon to be part of the great festival which is the Cowal Games. Started just a year or two before the pier was built, the event has blossomed and, especially if the weather is fine, attracts folk young and old from all walks of life. In the days before and after the last war one of the high-carrying turbines was held in reserve to transport the crowds of foot passengers across the firth some two thousand a time. Now the ferries do not have such capacities and the regulations regarding overcrowding on ships are much more strictly observed. The three 'streakers' are usually on duty

Scenes at the pier on a
busy afternoon evoke
memories of Dunoon's
halcyon days

The Caledonian Steam Packet Co Ltd

and are rostered to give a service every twenty minutes. The pipe bands
which are so much part of the Games tend now to travel by coach and
up to five such vehicles can be seen on the car deck at once. Thanks to
the consummate skill of the seamen, they are loaded and unloaded
with ease, despite the tight turn to disembark at the side-loading ramp
at Dunoon. In the evening, after the familiar march past down Argyll
Street, everyone seems to descend on Dunoon Pier at once and the
queue can stretch right up the gangway on to the Esplanade and out
to the Castle rocks. The pipes play and the onlookers sing, some in
tune and some in a more inebriated fashion. The *Waverley* casts off
fairly early for Glasgow, Cal Mac management are on the pier controlling
the embarkation procedure, ferries are lying off waiting to berth – even
the Rothesay ferry comes up to lend a hand – coaches manoeuvre with
adroitness on to the ferry's ramp and the crowds swarm up the new
broad gangways. By midnight the crowds are beginning to thin, by one
o'clock the last ferry leaves the berth. Perhaps Cowal Games Saturday
is the nearest approach today to the scene a hundred years ago during
the Glasgow Fair when the whole of the city seemed to empty and
descend on Dunoon by steamer every few minutes.

   Perhaps if we stand in the crowd seeping in the atmosphere and
looking up at the Victorian buildings little changed externally over the
century we can be forgiven for feeling just a little nostalgic.

Acknowledgements

A book like this one cannot be written without help and I acknowledge with a great deal of gratitude the assistance given by such individuals as Stuart Bryson of Dunoon & Cowal Heritage Trust; Mrs Marion Carmichael of the *Dunoon Observer*; Captain Robert L Hutchison, formerly of Caledonian MacBrayne; Iain MacArthur, steamer historian and author; Angus McLean, retired Dunoon solicitor and historian; Iain E Quinn of PSPS; Robert E Reid, Piermaster at Dunoon; Gregor Roy of Bookpoint; and the staff of Dunoon Library.

I also consulted the writings of the late David Robertson and George Stromier (whose article 'Dawdling at Dunoon' in *Clyde Steamers No 12* was invaluable) together with the Reviews of the Clyde River Steamer Club.

I am grateful too, to Derek Crawford for reading the manuscript and suggesting improvements and to Mrs MR McCrorie for reading the proofs. The photographs that are acknowledged in the captions were lent for this publication and I greatly appreciate the generosity of the donors; the others are from my own collection, the original photographers being largely unknown.

Ian McCrorie

Appendices

1. Steamers leave Dunoon: July 1897
(The opening of the south berth)

Departures are given Tuesday to Friday as Monday mornings and Saturday afternoons were appreciably different. The identity of some of the railway steamers is the result of intelligent guesswork and may not be accurate.

Time	Steamer	Company	Destination
0700	*Strathmore*	Williamson	Rothesay (papers)
0755	*Jupiter*	G & SW	Prince's Pier
0755	*Talisman*	NBSP	Craigendoran
0800	*Marchioness of Breadalbane*	CSP	Gourock
0822	*Mercury*	G & SW	Prince's Pier
0835	*Duchess of Rothesay*	CSP	Gourock
0915	*Redgauntlet*	NBSP	Craigendoran
0915	*Ivanhoe*	CSP	Various cruises
0915	*Culzean Castle*	GA & CS Co	Campbeltown
0930	*Columba*	MacBrayne	Ardrishaig
0930	*Duchess of Rothesay*	CSP	Arran via Kyles
0930	*Strathmore*	Williamson	Glasgow
0940	*Marchioness of Breadalbane*	CSP	Gourock
0945	*Lord of the Isles*	G & IS Co	Inveraray
1000	*Jupiter*	G&SW	Arran via Kyles
1000	*Dandie Dinmont*	NBSP	Craigendoran
1025	*Minerva*	G & SW	Arrochar
1105	*Marchioness of Lorne*	CSP	Gourock
1105	*Galatea*	CSP	Rothesay
1110	*Mercury*	G & SW	Kyles
1117	*Talisman*	NBSP	Rothesay
1122	*Lady Rowena*	NBSP	Arrochar
1150	*Victoria*	CS Ltd	Kyles (WX)
1203	*Redgauntlet*	NBSP	Rothesay
1210	*Meg Merrilies*	CSP	Gourock
1215	*Isle of Bute*	Buchanan	Rothesay
1217	*Marchioness of Breadalbane*	CSP	Rothesay
1310	*Talisman*	NBSP	Craigendoran

1315	*Isle of Arran*	Buchanan	Rothesay
1410	*Marchioness of Breadalbane*	CSP	Gourock
1410	*Meg Merrilies*	CSP	Rothesay
1449	*Talisman*	NBSP	Rothesay
1505	*Redgauntlet*	NBSP	Craigendoran
1510	*Galatea*	CSP	Gourock
1520	*Marchioness of Lorne*	CSP	Kyles
1520	*Glen Rosa*	G & SW	Kyles
1535	*Mercury*	G & SW	Prince's Pier
1555	*Meg Merrilies*	CSP	Gourock
1555	*Lady Rowena*	NBSP	Craigendoran
1610	*Columba*	MacBrayne	Glasgow
1610	*Iona*	MacBrayne	Ardrishaig
1620	*Strathmore*	Williamson	Rothesay
1630	*Talisman*	NBSP	Craigendoran
1650	*Jupiter*	G & W	Prince's Pier
1703	*Mercury*	G & SW	Rothesay
1708	*Galatea*	CSP	Rothesay
1712	*Redgauntlet*	NBSP	Rothesay
1725	*Isle of Arran*	Buchanan	Glasgow
1730	*Duchess of Rothesay*	CSP	Gourock
1800	*Dandie Dinmont*	NBSP	Craigendoran
1810	*Lord of the Isles*	G & IS Co	Greenock
1815	*Jupiter*	G & SW	Rothesay
1820	*Duchess of Rothesay*	CSP	Rothesay
1823	*Talisman*	NBSP	Rothesay
1840	*Isle of Bute*	Buchanan	Glasgow
1905	*Redgauntlet*	NBSP	Craigendoran
1908	*Minerva*	G & SW	Rothesay
1910	*Marchioness of Lorne*	CSP	Gourock
1915	*Culzean Castle*	GA & CS Co	Greenock
1928	*Dandie Dinmont*	NBSP	Kilmun
1930	*Glen Rosa*	G & SW	Prince's Pier
1955	*Strathmore*	Williamson	Gourock
2010	*Marchioness of Lorne*	CSP	Rothesay
2035	*Redgauntlet*	NBSP	Rothesay
2050	*Glen Rosa*	G & SW	Rothesay

Note that between 0915 and 0945 there are eight departures, three at 0915 and three at 0930: only one berth at Dunoon Pier was available. Note too that at 1105 and 1410 two CSP steamers are scheduled to depart at exactly the same time while at 1610 MacBrayne's *Columba* and *Iona* are both timetabled to leave. The G&SW Ayr Excursion steamer

Neptune has been omitted as her calls are irregular, as has the *Ivanhoe* on her return from her cruise and the cargo steamers, including Williamson's *Benmore* and *Sultana*. The *Marchioness of Breadalbane* and *Marchioness of Bute*, the *Glen Rosa* and *Minerva* and the *Redgauntlet* and *Talisman* were liable to interchange rosters.

Companies:

Culzean Castle:	Glasgow, Ayrshire & Campbeltown Steamboat Co. Ltd.
Lord of the Isles:	Glasgow & Inveraray Steamboat Co. Ltd.
Victoria:	The Clyde Steamers Ltd.

2. Steamers leave Dunoon: July 1937
(The building of the promenade balcony)

Departures are given Tuesday to Friday as Monday mornings and Saturday afternoons were appreciably different.

Time	Steamer	Company	Destination
0735	*Kenilworth*	LNER	Craigendoran
0752	*Mercury*	LMS	Gourock
0818	*Marmion*	LNER	Craigendoran
0823	*Duchess of Rothesay*	CSP (LMS)	Princes Pier
0910	*Kylemore*	WB	Glasgow
0913	*Jeanie Deans*	LNER	Various cruises
0920	*Duchess of Argyll*	CSP (LMS)	C'town/Inveraray
0920	*Duchess of Montrose*	CSP (LMS)	Various cruises
0930	*Caledonia*	CSP (LMS)	Arran via Kyles
0945	*Saint Columba*	MacBrayne	Ardrishaig
1000	*Juno*	CSP (LMS)	Gourock
1005	*Mercury*	LMS	Wms Bay/R'say
1010	*Kenilworth*	LNER	Craigendoran
1045	*Marmion*	LNER	Rothesay
1055	*Talisman*	LNER	Craigendoran
1100	*Waverley*	LNER	Arrochar
1110	*Duchess of Rothesay*	CSP (LMS)	Kyles
1215	*Queen Mary II*	WB	Arran Cruise
1225	*Juno*	CSP (LMS)	Rothesay
1230	*King Edward*	WB	Kyles, etc.
1230	*Marchioness of Lorne*	CSP (LMS)	Gourock
1305	*Marmion*	LNER	Craigendoran
1305	*Talisman*	LNER	Kyles
1345	*Queen-Empress*	WB	Cumbrae Circle
1350MTTh	*Eagle III*	WB	Lochgoilhead
1405	*Jupiter*	CSP (LMS)	Gourock
1430MThF	*Duchess of Montrose*	CSP (LMS)	Loch Goil Cruise

1430TF	*Mercury*	LMS	Rothesay
1440	*Marmion*	LNER	Rothesay
1505	*Kenilworth*	LNER	Craigendoran
1530	*Jupiter*	CSP (LMS)	Rothesay
1540	*Duchess of Rothesay*	CSP (LMS)	Gourock & Pr Pier
1610	*Saint Columba*	MacBrayne	Glasgow
1615TTh	*Mercury*	LMS	Millport
1630	*Kylemore*	WB	Rothesay
1645	*Marmion*	LNER	Craigendoran
1645MF	*Duchess of Montrose*	CSP (LMS)	Wms Bay/R'say
1710	*Waverley*	LNER	Rothesay
1713	*Duchess of Rothesay*	CSP (LMS)	Gourock
1725	*King Edward*	WB	Glasgow
1730	*Caledonia*	CSP (LMS)	Gourock & Pr Pier
1735TW	*Duchess of Montrose*	CSP (LMS)	Gourock
1750MTTh	*Eagle III*	WB	Glasgow
1800	*Talisman*	LNER	Craigendoran
1800	*Queen Mary II*	WB	Glasgow
1810	*Duchess of Argyll*	CSP (LMS)	Gourock
1820	*Duchess of Rothesay*	CSP (LMS)	Gourock
1830	*Marmion*	LNER	Rothesay
1905	*Waverley*	LNER	Craigendoran
1920	*Mercury*	LMS	Gourock & Pr Pier
2005	*Duchess of Rothesay*	CSP (LMS)	Rothesay

The CSP (LMS) Ayr Excursion steamer *Duchess of Hamilton* has been omitted, as her calls as irregular, as have the cargo steamers. Note that *Caledonia, Juno, Jupiter, Marchioness of Lorne, Mercury* and *Talisman* are new vessels since 1897. *Jupiter* and *Juno* changed rosters daily, as did *Kenilworth* and *Marmion*. On most days at least one steamer would be involved in an evening cruise.

Companies:

CSP (LMS): all steamers registered in the name of The Caledonian Steam Packet Co. Ltd. except for *Mercury*, which was owned directly by the LMS.

WB: Williamson-Buchanan Steamers (1936) Ltd, like the CSP a subsidiary of the LMS

3. Steamers leave Dunoon: July 1972
(The coming of the linkspan)

Time	Steamer	Destination
0725	*Glen Sannox*	Gourock
0835	*Glen Sannox*	Gourock
0910FX	*Queen Mary II*	Campbeltown, Inveraray, Arran
0910F	*Waverley*	Tarbert
0930	*Maid of Cumbrae*	Gourock
0935T	*Waverley*	Round the Lochs
1015	*Glen Sannox*	Gourock
1100	*Maid of Cumbrae*	Gourock
1120M	*Waverley*	Craigendoran
1130MX	*Maid of Argyll*	Craigendoran
1130Th	*Waverley*	Arrochar
1145	*Glen Sannox*	Gourock
1230	*Maid of Cumbrae*	Gourock
1310	*Maid of Argyll*	Rothesay & Millport
1315	*Glen Sannox*	Gourock
1325MWF	*Waverley* (QMII F)	Round Bute
1400	*Maid of Cumbrae*	Gourock
1445	*Glen Sannox*	Gourock
1445T	*Waverley*	Loch Goil
1530	*Maid of Cumbrae*	Gourock
1615	*Maid of Skelmorlie*	Gourock
1615	*Glen Sannox*	Gourock
1635T	*Waverley*	Largs & Rothesay
1700	*Maid of Cumbrae*	Gourock
1735	*Glen Sannox*	Gourock
1735Th	*Waverley*	Largs
1830	*Maid of Cumbrae*	Gourock
1845MTW	*Waverley*	Gourock (& Craigendoran)
1900	*Glen Sannox*	Gourock
1900 ca	*Queen Mary II*	Gourock
2030	*Glen Sannox*	Gourock

Maid of Argyll and *Maid of Skelmorlie* alternated daily Monday to Friday.

All vessels owned by The Caledonian Steam Packet Co. Ltd., now a subsidiary of the Scottish Transport Group.

Comparison:

In 1897, 65 or 66 calls were made by 21 or 22 vessels;

In 1937, 45 to 49 calls were made by 18 or 19 vessels;

In 1972, 24 calls were made by 6 vessels.

The staff of Dunoon pier, June 1997
(l to r) S Shelton. K Beattie (foreman), R E Reid (piermaster), D Stewart (assistant piermaster), S Greer, D Kent and P Lambert (assistant piermaster)